Table of Contents

Hospitality Motivations

The word 'hospitality' in the New Testament comes from two Greek words. The first word means 'love' and the second word means 'strangers.'- Nancy Leigh DeMoss. If you love people and the fast-paced hustle of serving and entertaining others, hospitality might be for you. Despite what the word means, if you are in the hospitality industry, there sure are days when it is hard to love the strangers that come through the doors. People in the hospitality industry scarcely have a moment to think or relax. There could be dozens of voicemail messages to deal with, dozens of people waiting to be served at the front counter, or piles of paperwork to take care of. It is usually always rushing go, go, go.

Hospitality is the world's largest and fastest-growing industry. A career in this dynamic field will introduce you to the world of service many times through travel. There are exciting tourist spots where you can land professionally, including and likely internationally. I have a saying that goes like this: *"once in hospitality, always in hospitality."* If you know people working in hospitality operations, can you think of many that went to other industries? I would bet not many. While hospitality is a broad field, it is divided into four major categories: guest relations, food and beverage, travel/tourism and entertainment.

"Hospitality means primarily the creation of free spaces where the stranger can enter and become a friend instead of an enemy. Hospitality is not to change people, but to offer them space where change can take place. It is not to bring men and women over to our side, but to offer freedom not disturbed by dividing lines." - Henri J.M. Nouwen. Below are other related inspirational hospitality quotes compiled by the writer Kim Campbell:

"Courteous treatment will make a customer a walking advertisement." - James Cash Penney

"The reason for our success is no secret. It comes down to one single principle that transcends time and geography, religion and culture. It's the Golden Rule - the simple idea that if you treat people well, the way you would like to be treated, they will do the same." - Isadore Sharpe

"The key is to set realistic customer expectations and then not to just meet them, but to exceed them - preferably in unexpected and helpful ways." - Sir Richard Branson

"To put it rather bluntly, I am not the type who wants to go back to the land; I am the type who wants to go back to the hotel." - Fran Lebowitz

"The great advantage of a hotel is that it is a refuge from home life." - George Bernard Shaw

"Entertaining doesn't need to be a difficult or daunting process. Throwing an unforgettable party doesn't require a ton of time or money; it just requires a little thought, creativity, and heart." - Maury Ankrum

"Travel is the only thing you buy that makes you (immediately) richer." - Unknown

"Your most unhappy customers are your greatest source of learning." - Bill Gates

"I have found out that there ain't no surer way to find out whether you like people or hate them than to travel with them." - *Mark Twain*

"I still enjoy traveling a lot. I mean, it amazes me that I still get excited in hotel rooms just to see what kind of shampoo they've left me." - *Bill Bryson*

"A hotel should relieve travelers of their insecurity and loneliness. It should make them feel warm and cozy." - Bill Kimpton

"You can excuse an ugly building if the staff deliver the right service (it's much nicer to have a combination of both things), but the staff at the end of the day are the service." - Rocco Forte

"The important thing is to engage guests in the hotel. Don't go in saying you know this and you know that, and this is the way it will be. Listening is critical to leadership, and so is staying authentic. You do that and you will get loyalty, and then your role as a leader will be easy." - Mark Hoplamazian

"Train people well enough so they can leave, treat them well enough so they don't want to." - Richard Branson

"In hospitality, there's always more to learn, and you're dealing with so many different types of people from all over the world every single day. You'll never know it all, and that can be humbling..." - Dwight Zahringer

"I tell our people all the time (that) 'success is never final,' and it isn't. It's a lot easier sometimes to get to the top than it is to stay there." - J. Willard Marriott

"Quality is never an accident. It is always the result of an intelligent effort." - John Ruskin

"Get your goals figured out first, then clearly articulate them to anyone that can impact them, and then figure out your recipe for success." - Dave Roberts

"Being on par in terms of price and quality only gets you into the game. Service wins the game." - Tony Allesandra

"Never say no when a client asks for something, even if it is the moon. You can always try, and anyhow there is plenty of time afterward to explain that it was not possible." - Cesar Ritz

"People will forget what you said, forget what you did, but people will never forget how you made them feel." - Maya Angelou

"Mighty proud I am that I am able to have a spare bed for my friends." - Samuel Pepys

"Hospitality is the key to new ideas, new friends, new possibilities. What we take into our lives changes us. Without new people and new ideas, we are imprisoned inside ourselves." - Joan Chittister

"There are no traffic jams along the extra mile." - Roger Staubach

"Our full humanity is contingent on our hospitality; we can be complete only when we are giving something away; when we sit at the table and pass the peas to the person next to us, we see that person in a whole new way." - Alice Waters

To change and improve ourselves or our current environments, we must first go to other places. And when we go, we will need hospitality, which is the friendly and generous reception and entertainment of guests, visitors, or strangers.

Following the table of contents, the goals of this material are to introduce views of what hospitality is in essence and its fundamental importance, provide reflections on its critical challenges, spark interest in people to start or continue being involved with hospitality, stimulate solving its obstacles by critically thinking and innovating, taking risks and engaging in expanding its boundaries.

The value of this material is in the way it is organized, its broad coverage of hospitality still presented with simplicity, and the way it discusses complex points with proper brevity. It does not have the intention of finding definitive answers to the challenges presented but pointing the readers in relevant directions to help them select their own areas of focus.

This book is a careful compilation of around ten years of engagement with hospitality, from pieces of studies, data and original reflections from personal experiences. It skips some basics that come from many hospitality books and business administration literature and brings to reflection very important but hidden advanced topics in hospitality that are not often deeply or critically discussed as they should be.

Hospitality is much more than businesses, although it is often seen through their lenses, and hospitality as a business is what made the industry so prominent. However, hospitality, historically and in essence, is much more than that and nonfinancial rewards are what also help people involved with hospitality to endure. Hospitality is broad and every sustainable business can be seen as a hospitality business, making or at least trying to make the life of people easier.

My life is hospitality because I chose to, earlier and continuously in life; however, I did not want to stay many years in day-to-day hospitality operations for reasons that will be described in this material, and that intrigued me because I know day-to-day operations are vital to the industry. I understand that what displeased me also affects many other people, and I wanted to help them to avoid those feelings.

As a teenager, I was introduced to hospitality and travel by my mother, which had a travel agency business for many years until the internet and online travel agencies crushed it. She also showed me that business and leisure, most times, can happen at the same time.

I chose to study and graduate in Business Administration from a good university and only towards the end of a five-year study of vast business literature I chose hospitality as a career path, naturally because many business disciplines were already applicable and useful to the hospitality industry, such as marketing, sales, finance, accounting, economics, strategy, entrepreneurship, logistics, efficient operations, psychology, human resources, legal and more. Also, the fact I had prior experiences from a related family business, knowledge of languages, visited many of the most famous cities in the world and good higher education, it made me believe I would have an edge in the industry, with greater chances of having an international career, which after I achieved and went to live in Orlando, one of the top tourism destinations in the world, becoming a businessman, consultant, entrepreneur and investor.

Before I completed 30 years old, I had visited many countries and stayed in all kinds of hospitality places where you sleep in a bed, such as resorts, hotels from 1 to 5 stars, hostels, camping, vacation rentals, timeshares and cruises. I also studied the subjects formally and their business models and worked providing most of their direct and ancillary products and services.

Imagine if we could live our entire life in nice hotels? All-inclusive resorts, such as Club Med, initially caught my attention because most of our human needs were attended to while there, including the offering of great socialization, not offered by other lodging or accommodation providers, except hostels, which overall blew my mind, and I decided I wanted to get involved with that as well.

Hospitality Characteristics

A society that can offer great hospitality to others can and often do it also for itself. When societies meet their basic needs, usually provided by good hospitality, it opens space for prosperity in other fields, such as innovation. Even though many argue innovation comes from necessity and hardships, which is also true, I believe it can also come from abundance because of the released resources, larger attention span, ease of primary concerns and provides comfort for people to relax and innovate. This is why many first-world countries are the most innovative ones, at least apparently. Places that offer great hospitality are also seem as friendly, open to others, and therefore, well accepted by many.

Many people that are involved with hospitality, especially the staff, do not like it though, and claim they do it out of necessity. One of the reasons why is that making people happy and satisfied on a constant basis is one of the most challenging (and not immediately rewarding) endeavors. It requires us to abdicate our selfishness and give more than taking, constantly. A hotelier /ˌôtelˈyā/ is a person who owns or manages lodging accommodations being usually involved in the long term. The key, in my view, is to understand that everybody involved with the industry do not need to surrender from their own happiness or from who they truly are, especially because many will better enjoy their hospitability if they feel we are being original and enjoy providing it in the acceptable personal frequency. It is also recommended patience and 'no pain, no gain' mentality, especially from younger generations, because the rewards will come later. In balancing this, the offer of great hospitality can be sustainably achieved from the personal level.

Hospitality is also making people feel physiologically comfortable, attending basic needs we all have, obvious as it sounds, such as providing quality air, water, food, shelter, rest, temperature control, hygiene and security. Those things hospitality endeavors must attend. Hospitable people that engage in hospitality businesses try to offer refuge to others from the endless discomforts of this world.

Some organizations, above physical needs, also endeavor to fulfill the psychological needs of customers, making them feel higher self-esteem and a sense of belongingness. Part of the way to achieve this is only via people (employees or other guests), but difficult to achieve and very difficult to scale. Guests' or customers' happiness tends to come at moments when all the physical and psychological needs are fulfilled. Hospitality businesses often struggle because guests have different tastes, and hospitality offers tend to be constant and inflexible to be scalable.

According to Peter Venison, in his book 100 Tips for Hoteliers, the way customers perceive the hospitality provided can be divided into dissatisfiers and satisfiers, usually, the dissatisfiers have to do with lacking to provide the basics, such as a clean sheet, hot water, door locks functioning, short wait times, even a beautiful architecture, etc. The satisfiers, on the other hand, have to do with the "software" or social aspects of the industry, such as compassion, kindness, warmth, love and caring. Staff who have gone the extra mile, have foreseen needs, and done something about them, raise the bar and reviews for their properties. These satisfiers are mostly things that do not cost much, as the hotel needs to identify who do it naturally and properly, empower that group and divide fairly schedules to stimulate more interactions of these employees with the customers.

Hospitality is most needed when people travel out of their comfort zones, and if you can help them attend to their needs faster, you will be compensated somehow. Hospitality is not only for traveling though but is needed everywhere when you go to the restaurant in your city, attend a class, visit your grandma's house, transport yourself and more. It can be offered greatly, not always in a luxurious way, but often times in an affordable and original way. Also, many businesses that provide services for travelers also please their local residents with their offers and vice versa.

Why do people travel? Usually, for leisure, business, education, relationships, start another life and a mix of all. There are many durations as well, such as one day, two days, a week, a month, a year, each one a very different trip, planned or unplanned. Humans chase nomadic lives and try to scape monotony, especially if they are between 25 and 34 years old; trends like the desire for access, not ownership, and remote work are fueling traveling and are here to stay with the help of the internet, transportation and technology.

Hospitality businesses, mainly lodging and accommodations, deal with an immensely vast array of subjects, and hoteliers need to have knowledge in areas such as:

- Strategy
- Real Estate
- Architecture
- Construction
- Design
- Maintenance
- Furnishings
- Fixtures
- Destination Marketing

- Logistics
- Customer Service
- Acting
- Housekeeping
- Laundry
- Security
- Food And Beverage
- Marketing
- Sales
- Revenue Management
- Finance
- Accounting
- Taxes
- Statistics
- Information Technology
- Sustainability
- Leadership
- Human Resources
- Legal
- Safety
- Economics
- Geopolitics
- Worldwide Culture
- Languages
- Sociology
- History
- Entertainment
- Leisure
- Storytelling
- Well-Being
- Events, and more

Due to the almost impossibility of accumulating such an array of knowledge and skills within one person or even one organization, hospitality businesses, owners and general managers must use specialized groups of individuals or outsource third-party firms. Due to this complexity, ownership is becoming more and more separated from management, and management, using outsourced service providers. However, owners, asset managers and general managers still need to know quite well all topics above.

Accommodations or lodging, transportation, entertainment, food and beverage and other things related to travel are estimated to be more than 10% of the world's gross domestic product and workforce, which is somehow a big deal, circulating around $3 trillion dollars. Hospitality accommodations alone, which is the focus of this material, is estimated $800 million or 27% of the industry.

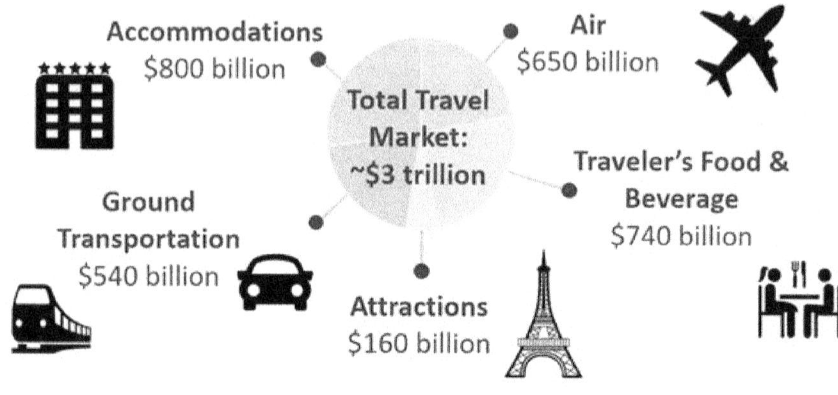

Source: Euromonitor, Phocuswright, internal estimates for 2019

In this material, when the term hotel is used, it can also mean other types of lodging accommodations such as resorts, limited-service hotels, full-service hotels, hostels, cruises, vacation rentals, timeshares, bed and breakfasts, and more. And $ values encountered are referred to U.S. dollars.

Hospitality Challenges

The challenges of hospitality are around the fact that it is mostly a complex, broad hybrid product and service intrinsically volatile and perishable, where if the service is not purchased that day or night, it cannot be stored and is lost, but the fixed costs and depreciation are still mostly incurred.

Whoever is involved with the hospitality industry needs to possess a vast array of knowledge from hard assets to soft people skills. There is a general perception that the hospitality industry, among a few others, is comprised of mostly low-level skilled workforce that naturally burns out fast, with shorter lengths of permanency in their jobs, which means high turnover. Also, when there is a strong demand for the product, it is not easy to adjust the prices fast enough and when the demand is low, it is not easy to cut expenses fast enough.

Even in the restaurant businesses, where the food and beverage are, at least perceived, as a product, not a service, a famous chef once said upscale restaurants are first environment, second service and only third the food or the product. In hotels, for example, the facilities and rooms are a product given temporary rights to usage. Services are intangible, do not characterize the transfer of ownership, and are evaluated very differently from customer to customer since experiences depend mostly on the customers' perspective. It is also mostly a Business to Consumer (B2C), not Business to Business (B2B), this last involving less volume and the decision power is in the hands of a few to convince to purchase your offers. Not to mention hospitality is a very competitive industry.

There is also an extensive perception, many times true, that hospitality is the riskiest type of real estate investment, which ultimately is what it is, mainly a real estate investment. When compared to land, residential, industrial and commercial real estate such as offices and retail, hospitality real estate is often the most capital intensive in the beginning and along its life stages, with longer return on investment, faster depreciation, difficult to sell and with heavier work and management daily supervision requirements.

Another major challenge is that the hospitality industry tends to be the first to be heavily and negatively affected by most economic, geopolitical or environmental crises and one of the last ones to recover from them. Traveling for most reasons happens with discretionary income, which is the money you have after paying taxes and other living expenses, examples of its use would be going out to dinner and movies, ordering tickets to a show, or going on vacations. In times of crisis, much less is available for those purposes. Hospitality caters to travelers but not all of them since it does not benefit much from migration crises, where those who are migrating do not have resources. Examples of such severe crises in the hospitality industry were observed during the 9/11 attacks and the infectious disease Covid-19. Other examples were portrayed by the movie Hotel Rwanda showing a social cohesion erosion in Africa and the Ukrainian migrations to Europe in 2022. As industry participants, how to be better prepared?

The Covid-19 pandemic around 2020 had an extreme negative impact on the airlines, cruises and hospitality industries, maybe among the top affected industries that first felt the impact, and then the latest to recover. The impact, despite being visible, is still difficult to fully measure, especially the permanent impact. These industries are known for having high fixed costs and cash flow disbursement obligations related to debt payments. Places that required proximity to other human beings had two or three years of barely any customers, such as airplanes, buses, hotels with elevators and hostels with their shared rooms, just to mention a few.

A lot has been written about the impacts of Covid-19 on the hospitality industry, however, it is worth emphasizing that the level of uncertainty related to hoteliers trying to forecast how long it would last was never seen before. The recovery is taking more than two years, which for certain businesses was fatal. The way these industries coped with the situation was by first laying off employees to a called skeleton crew, keeping only vital business functions operating, renegotiating contracts and leases, trying to sell assets and cutting fixed costs, all to extreme levels. Some businesses were able to survive with the help of government incentives. Many also are adapting to address trends that have become more visible, such as offering more wellness services and infrastructure for the rising number of remote workers.

However, the recovery has been quite strong due to the called accumulated pent-up demand from guests being constrained to travel during the pandemic. The level of disruption still lingers with labor shortages to cope with the high demand afterward. The resilience, flexibility and learning from the hardship that the hospitality industry had were astonishing and are helping it to adapt and move forward.

All the challenges mentioned above are difficult to overcome and having a pessimist mindset is not that difficult. Hospitality gave me many pleasures and memories in life on my own and with people, it also gave me financial independence and a way to help others properly. What intrigues me is how to overcome its challenges and make it more accessible. The industry organized the way it is nowadays is still a historically recent event and because of that presents opportunities. It appears that it all comes down to the fact that what is offered must be really that important for humanity and needs to continue, while still facing all these challenges, and that brings me optimism to pursue improvements. I heard recently that many smart engineers have the wrong mindset wired to improve things that should not even exist in the first place, it appears to me that this line of thought does not apply to hospitality.

Hospitality Higher Education

The higher university education in hospitality, its empirical studies, research, publication of books and academic articles on the topic are still a very recent phenomenon. The above is changing but is still in the early stages of reaching its full potential.

"Hospitality is almost impossible to teach. It's all about hiring the right people." - Danny Meyer. Many view the subject as only revolving around technical knowledge and applied on-the-job training, not supporting or understanding the importance of research and the strategic critical thinking approach to hospitality.

Many of the general business administration curriculum, which has several branches that hospitality education uses, already took leaps towards being more strategically centered or at least saw the importance of doing so. Even though many people involved with the hospitality industry lack extensive prior higher education, it does not mean they cannot understand, reflect, or even be invited to discuss in a deeper way what is this that affects their lives quite well. These are the people that must be studied. However, day-to-day operations are so intensive that they leave little time to see or think about the bigger picture or try new approaches.

Some people defend hospitality education as on-the-job mostly, not in the classroom or from readings. A combination of both, when possible, is ideal. It is important too, that even highly educated professionals spend time performing all kinds of hospitality roles in a quality rotational program through different departments. Their developed critical thinking skills can help to identify and innovate in areas of struggle for the business.

A bachelor's in hospitality management is a blend of business and hospitality courses. It is recommended a prior strong Business Administration education and fluency in as many different languages as possible. A vast traveling experience is also extremely desirable, staying in diverse types of lodging accommodations. It gives the person a strong base for working in the industry. Some programs emphasize more of the business side, such as marketing, operations, finance, strategy, human resources, logistics, basic laws, etc., other programs focus more on the hospitality side, such as customer service, food and beverage, real estate, related laws, etc.

There are many rankings of hospitality schools. The Best Hospitality and Hotel Management Schools in The World in 2022, according to the CEOWORLD Magazine and Sophie Ireland (just to give us an idea of schools available and not necessarily the exact order), is below. It is worth studying on your own the cities they are present and surrounding hospitality employment opportunities.

For example, at Cornel University in Ithaca, New York State, they have a strong real estate curriculum that is not easy to find in other schools. At the University of Central Florida Rosen College in Orlando, initially sponsored by the businessman, investor, and philanthropist Harris Rosen and where I had my master's degree in Hospitality, they have unique courses in timeshare or vacation ownership that are not found in other schools. Formal education in hospitality is evolving at a faster pace and is somehow recent. Although the top 10 schools do not change their ranking positions much, they likely will shift their rankings positions among themselves often. Interestingly is that the EHL École Hôtelière de Lausanne in Switzerland is not listed in this ranking and many times is consistently regarded as the best (and oldest) hospitality school in the world.

Rank	University	Country	Score
1	Nolan School of Hotel Administration (Cornell University)	USA	99.81
2	William F. Harrah College of Hospitality (University of Nevada, Las Vegas)	USA	98.38
3	School of Hospitality Business at Michigan State University	USA	95.95
4	Johnson & Wales University's College of Hospitality Management (COHM)	USA	95.56
5	UCF Rosen College of Hospitality Management (University of Central Florida)	USA	95.30
6	Oxford School of Hospitality Management	UK	95.19
7	School of Hospitality and Tourism Management at Fairleigh Dickinson	USA	94.98
8	Penn State School of Hospitality Management	USA	94.73
9	School of Hospitality Business Management at Washington State University	USA	94.71
10	Collins College of Hospitality Management at Cal Poly Pomona	USA	94.54
11	School of Hospitality Leadership (SHL) at University of Wisconsin	USA	94.42
12	Howard Feiertag Department of Hospitality and Tourism Management	USA	94.21
13	Fritz Knoebel School of Hospitality Management	USA	93.90
14	Institute of Hotel Management Catering Technology and Applied Nutrition - Chennai	India	93.57
15	Cecil B. Day School of Hospitality Administration	USA	93.56
16	School of Hospitality and Tourism Management in the Spears Oklahoma State University	USA	93.52
17	Les Roches	Switzerland	93.18
18	SAIT's School of Hospitality and Tourism	Canada	92.96
19	Hotelschool The Hague	Netherlands	92.86
20	School of Hotel and Restaurant Management at W. A. Franke College of Business	USA	92.37
21	Kendall College of Culinary Arts and Hospitality Management at National Louis University	USA	92.00
22	Hospitality & Tourism Management Department at Isenberg School of Management	USA	91.90
23	PolyU's School of Hotel and Tourism Management	Hong Kong	91.85
24	Jonathan M. Tisch Center of Hospitality	USA	91.37
25	School of Hospitality and Tourism Management at University of Surrey	UK	90.97
26	College of Merchandising, Hospitality and Tourism at University of North Texas	USA	90.82
27	Zuyd University of Applied Sciences, Maastricht	Netherlands	90.80
28	Hospitality Management (HM) Program at The University of Alabama	USA	90.31
29	Cesar Ritz Colleges	Switzerland	90.30
30	Culinary Institute of America	USA	90.27
31	RIT's Saunders College of Business	USA	90.16
32	Hotel Institute Montreux	Switzerland	89.92

33	Barcelona School of Tourism, Hospitality and Gastronomy	Spain	89.92
34	College of Hospitality at Johnson & Wales University	USA	89.83
35	Pace's Lubin School of Business	USA	89.72
36	Culinary Arts Academy	Switzerland	89.51
37	Saxion University of Applied Sciences, Apeldoorn	Netherlands	89.45
38	Culinary Institute of New York (CINY)	USA	89.34
39	State University of New York College at Plattsburgh	USA	88.89
40	Nanyang Institute of Management's School of Tourism and Hospitality	Singapore	88.88
41	Sejong University	South Korea	88.86
42	Swiss Hotel Management School	Switzerland	88.62
43	Hotel Management School Geneva	Switzerland	88.58
44	Emirates Academy of Hospitality Management	UAE	88.57
45	Glion Institute	Switzerland	88.50

Hospitality Books, Articles, Movies, TV-Series and Websites

A series of hospitality books, academic articles, movies, tv-series, and websites should be enjoyed by those who want to continue engaging with the subject. This list is far from complete, but it is comprised of relevant and advanced materials that came first to mind and have been a source of continuous inspiration.

<u>Books</u>
- Great American Hoteliers
- Valuation of Hotels for Investors
- Uniform System of Accounting for the Lodging Industry
- The Negotiation and Administration of Hotel Management Contracts
- Cornell School of Hotel Administrations Cutting Edge Thinking and Practice
- There are many introductory and general books written, mostly by professors of hospitality schools, that are recommended in the initial stages. Many follow general business curriculums adding case studies in hospitality.

<u>Academic Articles and Journals</u>
Academic articles are the best way to find and deep dive into valuable literature about specific topics in hospitality you can search for that are on the edge of knowledge advancements. Many are not easy to read and contain technical languages to support methodic research and conclusions. Google Scholar is one of the most excellent sources for finding peer-reviewed articles from respected journals. Articles are many times the best source of knowledge, pretty much in most subjects or keywords you are researching. It is recommended to know how to find and access these articles and journals by conducting proper searches that do not filter out valuable content. In order to find full texts of articles via Google Scholar, you can Advance your Search in several ways, being careful with the selections of your keywords. Ensure to use Boolean Operators such as AND, OR, and quotation marks "" to search exactly, dates of articles, author-related articles, peer-reviewed, number of citations and more. However, to access full texts, students might have to go to libraries or obtain online permission from university domains.

<u>Movies</u>

- Hotel Rwanda
- The Grand Budapest Hotel
- Best Exotic Marigold Hotel
- Hotel Transylvania Cartoon Series
- Bad Times at the El Royale
- The Florida Project
- Bobby

<u>TV-Series</u>

- Hotel Impossible - Several Seasons

<u>Websites</u>

- hospitalitynet.org
- Skift.com
- str.com
- hvs.com

Hotel Types

There are many types of hotels and not a specific standard convention of how to group them. Usually, they are separated by what they offer, such as the number of rooms, services rendered, location, room types, layout, restaurants on-site, what is included in the price, etc.

Hotel types are usually known:

- Hostels
- Bed and Breakfasts
- Inns
- Motels
- Independent Hotels
- Chain Hotels
- Eco Hotels
- Casino Hotels
- Conference Hotels
- Boutique Hotels
- All-Suites
- Extended Stays
- Resorts
- Cruises
- All-Inclusive, and more

Ironically, after years of studies and personal experiences in *all* kinds of hotel types above, I am fond and have particular interests in hotel types of the farthest opposite spectrums, hostels and all-inclusive.

Hostels, due to their combination of central locations, being trendy for younger solo travelers, their shared rooms component and fun social areas, sometimes guest kitchens, and affordability.

All-inclusive resorts, specific ones, not most, due to the immersive scenarios they provide to attend most human needs, specifically from Maslow's hierarchy of human necessities pyramid perfective, which will be detailed later. All-inclusive resorts offer what is needed to foster the temporary achievements of higher-level human goals, such as the feeling of achieving high senses of belongingness, self-esteem, self-actualization, vitality, self-sufficiency, authenticity, playfulness, and meaningfulness.

When with the proper combination and subset of guests and staff, depending on each guest's personal preferences, plus gorgeous temperature and nature, the subtle reliefs offered of not having to pay on the spot for food, beverages, entertainment, child supervision, activities, equipment, the practices of sports and more, the all-inclusive resort overall offer proposition, when properly delivered, is a powerful way to solidify great experiences and lasting memories.

Hospitality Developments – Demand, Offer and Costs

How to define in which locations to be present with your lodging accommodations? It depends on demand and offer, plus inner motivations. The demand and the offer can and should be segmented to add lower or higher-cost lodging accommodations to the market.

If the *expected* demand is *perceived* to not be strong enough to add new lodging accommodations of the type *you can* offer, there is a better option to *acquire current* accommodations and keep them as it is or reposition them if potential is identified. Even if there is a belief that the target areas are not initially attractive, depending on the price to develop, it can be worth the risk-taking to penetrate the market this way by acquisitions without adding market inventory.

There are strong arguments that the offer should follow the demand. However, the demand is not always present, and it can be *created.* That applies especially to infrastructure projects like hotels. They are capital intensive and riskier, but they can pay off.

The personnel's or company's desire to have lodging accommodations in the most sought and trendy cities and locations is a risky bias to be carefully analyzed. Data is not always accurate, but the world's most visited cities by international travelers per year such as Bangkok (23 million), Paris (19 million), London (19 million), Dubai (16 million) and New York (13 million) are just examples. Many cities receive mostly national travelers from within their countries too like Orlando. Sometimes, however, developing in less sought and underserved locations can pay off even more from other perspectives. Businesses can benefit from more local community support in remote locations, easier access to land and lower development costs, easier access to personnel, taxes incentives and more. In this last scenario, more offers can lead to more demand, or at least wait sustainably for the demand to come.

A great part of the *expectations* of demand and assessment of current and expected future offers is a guessing game and will require risk-taking at levels the developer can support. The development of hospitality real estate has several high barriers, including high costs and competition, which are also barriers to entry for future competitors. The rise of single home vacation rentals is also imposing another threat dragging part of the demand.

Some traditional and non-traditional ways to forecast demand are many and depend on the timeframe, which for hotel development usually is ten years or more. A big factor in forecasting demand for lodging accommodations or other hospitality businesses is also predicting the overall destination offers of new attractions and infrastructure, plus safety, geopolitics, and economic environments.

Regarding the offer, it requires a market study to identify the current hotel inventory and the pipeline of new hotels, their locations, facilities, and rate ranges. Past and current occupancy and ADR of present hotels can also be obtained despite difficult, including their past and current online reviews volume and levels.

Ultimately, looking at both expected demand and offer characteristics, it becomes easier to see opportunities for specific locations and lodging accommodation types that are underserved. Hotel developers, as a last resort and in most cases, though, can always decide to decline, hold, or postpone new developments in the target areas and dedicate more time to research.

Per an article written in Fixr.com and reviewed in 2022 by Adam Graham, the *costs to build hotels* in the USA, as a reference, are below. These costs will vary a lot based on other countries' conditions:

Build a **100 rooms** Hotel Average Cost by Project Range:

Low – $7.5M - 2-story motel
Average – $22.1M - 3-star hotel in a suburban area
High – $60M - 5-star luxury hotel in an urban area

Hotel Type	Cost per **sq.ft.** in Rural Area	Cost per **sq.ft.** in Urban Area
Motel	$134 - $170	$180 - $234
3-Star	$190 - $245	$250 - $375
4-Star	$260 - $345	$350 - $410
5-Star	$332 - $400	$400 - $550
Guest House	$100 - $500	
Boutique Hotel	$190 - $550	
Casino	$300 - $550	
Resort	$300 - $550	

Hotel Type	Average Cost **per Room** to Build
Motel	$75,000
3-Star	$221,000
4-Star	$318,200
5-Star	$604,200

There are very few actual requirements regarding the size of a hotel room. The average size of a hotel room in the USA for a standard hotel is around 330 sq.ft.

Breakdown	Percent of Total Project Cost
Opening Expenses	3%
Furniture and Fixtures	9%
Land	10% - 21%
Soft Costs (Non-Construction Fees)	12%
Hard Costs (Material, Construction)	55% - 66%

Hard costs are construction-related expenses. These may include building or refurbishing an existing building. This includes the material and the labor needed to construct and finish the site. Hard costs include the finish materials, such as flooring and drywall, and basic construction materials, like concrete and steel. Because this group includes a range of materials and encompasses new builds and refurbishment of existing properties, the cost is 55% to 66%. Soft costs are non-construction-based fees. This includes the architect and interior designer fees, draftsman, structural engineers, and other things like maintenance, insurance, permits, taxes, and other related costs to build that are not a specific material or visible in the finished build. Soft costs average out to around 12% of your total budget.

It is common to work with a hotel builder or contractor specializing in this type of commercial build. Builders and contractors may charge up to $150 to $250 an hour for their services. In addition, you will likely need the services of the following professionals:

- Architect - $150 - $400/hour
- Interior Designer - $75 - $450/hour
- Concrete workers - $110/cubic yard
- Plumber - $45 - $200/hour
- Electrician - $50 - $100/hour
- Painter - $50/hour
- Flooring installer - $5 - $20/sq.ft.
- Carpenters - $90/hour
- HVAC technicians - $50 - $70/hour
- Structural engineers - $100 - $500/hour
- Tile installers - $5 - $10/sq.ft.
- Landscapers - $45 - $75/hour

A hotel can be managed in a way that brings it to breakeven in the first three years. Some though forecast returns only after 10 years. An excellent case is a breakeven after three years. Then there are an additional three years when the finances should be okay. And then, after seven years, it should start making good profits, and that is considered a good scenario.

Destination Marketing

Destination Marketing, especially in tourism, is meant to drive, increase or change demand for a specific destination, such as a city or country, via research, advertising and communication techniques with the focus on bringing potential external consumers or mainly visitors. It can also attract investors, businesses, new residents, university students and skilled labor force.

For local hospitality providers such as hotels, restaurants, entertainment venues, theme parks, convention centers, casinos, sports arenas, etc., providing a positive image of their locations are critical to their future. Destinations compete for external resources and collection of taxes, and many of these aspects of this competition happen in the marketing field, where advertises can shape the image and positioning they want to convey.

The image people have of a certain destination can be driven by news, friends and more, and it can be positive or negative. The areas of focus usually are entertainment options, costs, type of visitors, safety, weather, etc. The way those destinations convey their desired image costs funds to create and frequently update websites, advertise using several channels such as TV commercials, newspapers, magazines ads, social media ads, such as Facebook, Instagram and TikTok.

These costs usually are funded by local governments and non-profit organizations. They take the initiative to fund those efforts because attracting exterior resources increases tax collections and generates jobs and revenues for local businesses. These extra exterior resources are many times welcome, like when you are exporting an item, but actually, from within your location, the reason why tourism and hospitality are very beneficial to societies when sustainable.

Being attentive to the negative sides of over tourism apart, local families, businesses and government should generally strongly support hotels, since they create benefits to all in several areas, such as maintenance of jobs, generation of revenue from guests outside the region, improvement of local image, house and business values among other benefits.

The way to fund the costs of promoting a destination comes from a local collection of taxes and private companies that usually contribute through a non-mandatory fixed or variable amount depending on the size or their businesses. If the amount to fund is variable based on hotels revenues from example, which makes more sense since it should be a direct benefit of the actions of destination marketing, it becomes more difficult to ensure the proper amounts are being transferred by each business.

All hospitality providers should be stewards and adequately contribute funds since their regions tend to benefit overall from the efforts of destination marketing.

It is not always easy also to ensure certain associations are properly using the collected funds, as happens with many non-profit organizations. Most of these destination marketing agencies have the monopoly on representing the destination, which in a certain way makes sense to unify the image that is being conveyed, however, due to this reason, they might get complacent and comfortable in their monopoly position.

It is important to offer transparency, governance and compliance to donors and listen to them on which type of positioning they think would be better for their locations and which channels to use to promote it, including their costs. Plus, disclose the salaries of the personnel involved in managing the non-profit and its major suppliers. It is also recommended these associations to be independently audited to provide proper due diligence if their expenses are being reasonably allocated. It should follow the guidance of its independent board of directors from hospitality businesses that rotate seats often and are funding those efforts.

Finally, it is also recommended that the results of such destination marketing efforts need to be independently measured, with the number of visitors and comparisons from airport data and local governments not directly involved with the destination marketing agency.

Hospitality Marketing

To set hospitality businesses successfully apart from the competition, attract customers and make them loyal, the areas of focus in hospitality marketing should be:

- Product (Segment, Service and Facilities) - Position properly in terms of the competition.

- Location - This is one of the most important.

- Price - Greatly managed by the Revenue Management process. Not all customers are price sensitive.

- Online Reviews - Items that are mostly measured are Cleanliness, Staff, Safety, Location, Facilities, Comfort and others. They are tracked by each Online Travel Agency and must be constantly compared with the competition, also in terms of volume.

- Online Travel Agencies (OTAs) - Commissions can be between 15% to 20% of sales from those channels. Sales from OTAs can easily represent 65% to 90% of sales and from the marketing standpoint, it is extremely important to properly position with quality pictures and their order of presentations, rates, reviews and descriptions to achieve adequate and attractive search results ranking positions by specific sorting or filtering combinations desires. These OTAs also offer additional marketing promotional programs designed to boost your visibility and conversion rates that many times bring more returns than other marketing channels.

- Direct Website - An attractive, updated and easy-to-use website, that is responsive to different devices' screen sizes is a must investment. It serves to attract more direct commission-free sales, which should always be a goal. Proper Search Engine Optimization (SEO) is important to ensure your website contains keywords that will make it rank higher in Google Search and Google Hotels, plus other metasearch engines.

- Paid Promotion Channels - Online such as Facebook, Instagram, Google Ads Keyword and TikTok. The way to measure the results of campaigns is to track impressions, clicks and measure conversion prices. Plus, other options of paid promotions are in magazines, TV commercials, other related website mentions or banners such as airlines and travel blogs, events sponsorships, PR firms, trade-offs with writers, billboards, etc.

- Non-Paid Promotion Channels - word of mouth, free social media postings, blog mentions, email blasts, interview mentions, etc.

Hospitality Revenue Management

The art and science of revenue management in hotels are to try to sell beds at the right time, to the right guests and for the right price, constantly.

Revenue management is applicable not only to hotel rooms but also to restaurants, event spaces, sport courts and more. In the case of beds or hotel rooms, the main goal is usually to increase the RevPAR, which is the revenue per available room. First, they try to increase the ADR, which is the average daily rate measured by total room revenue divided by the number of rooms sold, however, if the ADR increases too much, revenue managers, most of the time, affect the occupancy negatively.

The revenue per available room (RevPAR) is obtained by multiplying the average daily rate (ADR) in a specific period by the occupancy percentage of that same period. For example, if the ADR was $100 and the occupancy was 80%, it means the RevPAR was $80. The goal of the revenue manager is to increase the RevPAR or by increasing the ADR or by increasing their occupancy. The art and the difficulty are really to properly balance how much more you can charge with your rates without negatively affecting much the occupancy.

Usually, revenue managers try to forecast the demand, forecast the supply or competitive offers and forecast the cancelation rates to then define their proper inventory availability and establish pricing, always attentive to not sell too cheap earlier or risk being too expensive last-minute.

Below is an example of how to look at the supply forecast:

Construction Pipeline by Market									
Market	Existing Inventory	Under Construction		Final Planning		Planning		Active Pipeline	
	As of September 2022	Rooms	% of Existing	Rooms	% of Existing	Rooms	% of Existing	Rooms	% of Existing
Top 25 Markets	**1,811,343**	**63,113**	**3.5%**	**57,504**	**3.2%**	**102,195**	**5.6%**	**222,812**	**12.3%**
Atlanta, GA	110,337	4,469	4.1%	5,458	4.9%	6,869	6.2%	16,796	15.2%
Boston, MA	62,730	1,407	2.2%	1,408	2.2%	1,888	3.0%	4,703	7.5%
Chicago, IL	121,247	2,175	1.8%	2,426	2.0%	4,724	3.9%	9,325	7.7%
Dallas, TX	97,183	4,533	4.7%	6,218	6.4%	7,812	8.0%	18,563	19.1%
Denver, CO	58,203	2,082	3.6%	2,871	4.9%	3,847	6.6%	8,800	15.1%
Detroit, MI	46,761	2,343	5.0%	2,813	6.0%	2,296	4.9%	7,452	15.9%
Houston, TX	97,947	2,816	2.9%	3,906	4.0%	3,623	3.7%	10,345	10.6%
Los Angeles, CA	114,644	3,182	2.8%	5,388	4.7%	9,145	8.0%	17,715	15.5%
Miami, FL	65,011	3,106	4.8%	2,393	3.7%	9,978	15.3%	15,477	23.8%
Minneapolis, MN	48,275	583	1.2%	471	1.0%	434	0.9%	1,488	3.1%
Nashville, TN	56,448	3,181	5.6%	3,263	5.8%	5,332	9.4%	11,776	20.9%
New Orleans, LA	41,055	668	1.6%	2,422	5.9%	566	1.4%	3,656	8.9%
New York, NY	127,091	12,000	9.4%	671	0.5%	2,642	2.1%	15,313	12.0%
Norfolk, VA	38,180	691	1.8%	281	0.7%	1,062	2.8%	2,034	5.3%
Oahu Island, HI	30,330	627	2.1%	544	1.8%	1,440	4.7%	2,611	8.6%
Orange County, CA	59,953	1,551	2.6%	869	1.4%	1,981	3.3%	4,401	7.3%
Orlando, FL	136,021	2,906	2.1%	2,828	2.1%	7,068	5.2%	12,800	9.4%
Philadelphia, PA	52,369	858	1.6%	1,403	2.7%	3,152	6.0%	5,413	10.3%
Phoenix, AZ	69,239	4,558	6.6%	3,077	4.4%	7,449	10.8%	15,084	21.8%
San Diego, CA	64,641	1,747	2.7%	2,361	3.7%	2,774	4.3%	6,882	10.6%
San Francisco, CA	55,338	1,009	1.8%	836	1.5%	3,952	7.1%	5,797	10.5%
Seattle, WA	50,613	1,608	3.2%	2,079	4.1%	2,271	4.5%	5,958	11.8%
St. Louis, MO	41,514	838	2.0%	1,304	3.1%	1,070	2.6%	3,212	7.7%
Tampa, FL	52,828	1,309	2.5%	979	1.9%	3,628	6.9%	5,916	11.2%
Washington, D.C.	113,385	2,866	2.5%	1,237	1.1%	7,192	6.3%	11,295	10.0%

Source: Deutsche Bank Supply Monitor (10/22)
Note: existing supply metrics exclude closed hotels at the time of the report.

The revenue manager should also be looking at the booking windows, or lead time, which show how far in advance the guests book from their arrival date. With this information, they can gauge if their occupancy levels are ideal, adjusting their rates up or down. Guests who book at the last minute often tend to pay higher rates since they likely are booking in a rush and hotels can take advantage of it by increasing their prices at the last minute. One of the big questions is how many rooms you should try to have available last minute at higher rates without running the risk of not selling them in a timely matter for each specific night. Other times, revenue managers offer last-minute rate reductions if their occupancy is low to try to attract more guests.

Average Length of Stay and Lead Time By Segment Q3 2022				
	LOS	Δ Vs. '19	Lead Time	Δ Vs. '19
Luxury	2.1	1.0%	37.7	-3.8%
Upper Upscale	1.8	1.7%	37.8	15.1%
Upscale	2.0	6.7%	29.5	23.2%
Upper Midscale	1.9	6.9%	24.4	34.3%
Midscale	2.1	8.3%	16.6	31.4%
Economy	3.3	40.2%	6.3	-13.5%

Source: Kalibri Labs

Note the revenue management tasks become increasingly complex as more room types the hotel has, such as double rooms, king bed rooms, shared rooms with individually sold single bunk beds, suites, presidential suites, etc. It is also important to define the best mix of room types and bed arrangements and, if possible, adapt to market demands assuming the system edits will not be that detrimental.

Currently, there are technologies that help considerably in revenue management tasks. For example, there are systems that automatically change rates based on parameters pre-defined by the revenue manager based on the occupancy levels, therefore the hotel does not miss the opportunity to quickly increase rates if the occupancy is picking up fast, the system alerts or adjusts automatically and distributes to all online travel agencies in real-time the new rates.

The same systems also help revenue managers to track the time competitors are changing their future rates in different OTAs and alert or automatically apply rate changes to the hotel's rates. For example, if the competitors increase or decrease their rates, the system then adjusts the hotel's rates automatically in the same proportion or to the same amount to match if those are the desired parameters. An important major influence in defining rates is, of course, the competition and how the hotel wants to be positioned in the search results of online travel agencies when sorted by lowest to the higher rate.

There are marketing theories though that defend prices are not the most important aspect when customers are deciding on a purchase.

An important aspect of their revenue management is to properly anticipate holidays and large events that can impact on the hotel's occupancy. There is a risk that the hotel will be selling at cheap rates and misses the opportunity of actually waiting for a bit more to sell that same room last minute to guests that would be paying higher rates in a rush. Therefore, it is important to have a calendar in advance with established and updated important dates in advance to then set up higher rates as soon as possible so the hotel does not miss opportunities.

It is very important to see the competitive set and how they are performing in terms of RevPAR, occupancy and ADR. Not always are the data easily available. Usually, it is available grouped without specified individual competitor hotels via consulting companies that sell reports. A major provider called STR can provide, at a cost, frequent reports of your competitive set.

Also, several OTA websites, such as Booking.com and Expedia, provide great analytics data to compare your performance.

To understand which events will impact your occupancy, it depends if you cater primarily to families, solo travelers, business travelers, etc. So many event types, such as sports events, conventions and concerts, will affect hotels differently depending on how they are positioned regarding the demographics they intended to attract or are already attracting.

Revenue management tactics will depend on the objectives that the hotel has regarding balancing rates and occupancy. For example, some hotels might want to pursue a higher occupancy because that may generate ancillary revenues at restaurants, retail stores, parking or via upselling services and products such as towels, vending machines, etc. However, high occupancy will bring more costs, such as utilities, maintenance and staff burn-out to check-in and check-out guests, plus housekeeping having to clean more rooms and public areas. On the other hand, there are several hotels that apply really high rates because they believe customers will pay whatever it is needed because they might be looking for that specific location, that specific hotel brand and did not shop much around last minute. It all depends on what are the main objectives of the hotel.

Also, keep in mind the occupancy depends on the amount and quality of marketing the hotel is doing. Revenue managers, therefore, need to be aligned with the marketing team to adjust rates for extra demand generated by their actions, and usually, that demand comes in the form of direct sales via the hotel's direct websites, which saves around 15% to 20% in commissions typically paid to OTAs.

As a last thought, in my view, the best way to measure the performance of the revenue managers is through the RevPAR historical comparisons from the prior month and the same month in previous years.

Online Travel Agencies and Metasearch Engines

Per the Big Book of OTAs, distributed by the property management system company Cloudbeds in 2022, love them or not, online travel agencies (OTAs) play a critical role in every hotel's distribution strategy. According to Phocuswright's 2020 research report, OTAs captured roughly 64% of online hotel & lodging bookings and have the visibility and marketing power that most individual properties cannot achieve on their own. Most of the content of this chapter is extracted as it is from this publication.

Working with OTAs isn't just a matter of signing up and hoping for the best. To take advantage of the opportunities and avoid the pitfalls, hoteliers need to actively manage their listings, pricing, and inventory, plus take a strategic approach to online distribution.

If done correctly, adopting the right OTAs as part of your distribution strategy can actually help drive direct bookings through the "billboard effect." Building a comprehensive channel mix incorporating different types of OTAs will ensure you reach your target audience and secure a steady stream of reservations.

In the Metasearch area, Google Hotel Search has disrupted the online travel industry, changing how travelers book their vacations. When a traveler enters a property name into Google, the site will return a list of hotel rates from various OTAs on which the property is listed. Clicking on a rate will take a traveler directly to that OTA to book.

In 2021, Google introduced free booking links, allowing an individual property to list their direct rates within the Google Hotel search box for free. In 2022, this initiative was expanded to include free booking links in both Google Search and Maps, meaning that properties now have an added way to capture direct bookings at multiple points on the Google platform commission-free.

In the late 1990s, OTAs began to emerge with Priceline.com (now Booking Holdings), Expedia Groups (as a division of Microsoft), and Ctrip (now Trip.com) leading the way. These OTAs changed how travel planning was done by aggregating information from across the internet into one place for travelers to compare options, pricing, reviews, and more.

Today, many travelers begin their journey on OTAs during the "dreaming phase" of travel. They use OTAs as a storefront to see what's available on the market. At this point in their travel journey, they are looking for inspiration and are open to various ideas, activities, and accommodations. Search activity is broad and destination oriented. In the planning stage, travelers use OTAs to narrow down their options, looking at factors such as amenities, pricing, and reviews. According to Yieldify, travelers spend on average more than four months researching their trip before departure and visit 38+ websites throughout this period. Properties must be listed on a wide variety of channels to increase their visibility and chances of conversion, plus ensure their direct websites are designed in a way that also leads to conversions. Monitoring of the number of website visits compared to direct bookings in the same period is valuable. Several analyses of demographics and areas of most clicks of your direct website visitors can help to adjust tactics for more direct booking conversions.

When booking, travelers will often go directly to a property's website after seeing them on multiple OTAs. This phenomenon called "The Billboard Effect" was first documented in 2009 by the Cornell Center for Hospitality Research and is still relevant today. A 2017 Cornell study found that properties connected to 7+ channels had a 20% increase in direct bookings as travelers became more aware of these properties and trusted their legitimacy.

Discount and deal-centric advertising campaigns help shape consumer notions that OTAs are the best place to book. Booking.com alone spent over $3.8 billion on marketing in 2021. Expedia and Booking.com both spent roughly $6 million on Super Bowl Ads.

A channel mix is the selection of OTAs and distribution channels that a property connects to. With the hundreds of online channels available today, properties should prioritize choosing channels that align with their brand and attract visitors who they've identified to be in their target market.

Under the agency model, one of the most common models used by OTAs, they act as an agent, passing reservations booked by customers to hotels and receiving a commission in return. Commissions between 15% to even 25% in total (most have been 15%) can either be paid at the time of booking or after an agreed-upon time, such as during the check-out month.

Naturally, as hoteliers increase the number of channels their properties are connected to, they will also collect more reviews. Positive online reviews are one of the best tools to convert travelers into guests. On the other hand, poor reviews will negatively impact the business. Therefore, hoteliers should develop a strategy to manage their online reputation. Sending out post-stay surveys to gauge guest satisfaction can give them an opportunity to identify and resolve issues before they get bad reviews and also help to recognize guests who are willing to leave a positive review.

Globally and regionally, the highest revenue generating OTAs in 2022 are below:

Rank	OTA
1	Booking.com
2	Expedia
3	Airbnb
4	Hostelworld
5	Agoda
6	Vrbo
7	Hotelbeds
8	Trip.com
9	Despegar / Decolar
10	Traveloka

USA

Rank	OTA
1	Booking.com
2	Expedia
3	Airbnb
4	Hostelworld
5	Vrbo
6	Agoda
7	HotelTonight
8	HRS
9	Hotelbeds
10	Google Hotel Search

LATAM

Brazil

Rank	OTA
1	Booking.com
2	Expedia
3	Airbnb
4	CVC
5	Despegar / Decolar
6	Hostelworld
7	Hotelbeds
8	Pricetravel
9	Agoda
10	Vrbo

Colombia

Rank	OTA
1	Airbnb
2	Booking.com
3	Expedia
4	Coliving
5	Hotelbeds
6	Tripadvisor Vacation Rentals
7	Hostelworld
8	Vrbo
9	Glamping Hub
10	Despegar / Decolar

Mexico

Rank	OTA
1	Booking.com
2	Expedia
3	Airbnb
4	Hostelworld
5	Despegar / Decolar
6	Pricetravel
7	Hotelbeds
8	Keytel
9	HotelTonight
10	Mr & Mrs Smith

Europe

Portugal

Rank	OTA
1	Booking.com
2	Airbnb
3	Hostelworld
4	Expedia
5	Hotelbeds
6	Agoda
7	Mr & Mrs Smith
8	Surf Holidays
9	HRS
10	Keytel

Spain

Rank	OTA
1	Booking.com
2	Airbnb
3	Hostelworld
4	Expedia
5	Hotelbeds
6	Agoda
7	Keytel
8	Dorms.com
9	Hostelsclub
10	HRS

UK

Rank	OTA
1	Booking.com
2	Airbnb
3	Expedia
4	Hostelworld
5	Agoda
6	Hotelbeds
7	Mr & Mrs Smith
8	Vrbo
9	Tripadvisor VR
10	Reconline

In my opinion, OTAs are beneficial to both guests and lodging accommodation providers. However, competition should be vastly stimulated in the sector to avoid the concentration of power in increasing commissions. Also, more transparency needs to be provided by OTAs to lodging accommodation providers when charging additional commissions, usually 10%, for guests who book packages that include flights and cars and better show the benefits of offering those discounted rate plans.

Metasearch engines, like Google Hotels, are beneficial to both guests and lodging accommodation providers and are being naturally supported since they stimulate direct bookings and still offer many of the benefits OTAs offer, such as exposure, online reviews and other comparisons.

Hotel Ownership Structures and Characteristics

Uncovering grouped statistics about hotel ownership is not an easy task in any country. Data, as in many cases, is mostly available in the USA. Hotel valuations and investment are also very hard, with many barriers, and only the privileged have access to endeavor in this industry as owners.

The basic understanding that lenders or banks usually lend around 50% to 80% of initial capital for construction or acquisitions and that owners typically do not manage the most complex hotels (Marriott, for example, owns very few hotels), helps to understand who hotel owners are, how they get there, the importance of their relationship with lenders and hotel managers plus other overall characteristics.

How to know what are the ownership and management structures of a hotel? Knowing the ownership structure is not easy. It can be easier, though, to identify if a branded hotel is franchised or managed by a hotel company since each hotel must have a plaque in the reception that explicitly discloses that, as it is a legal requirement. If you are not looking to leave the comfort of your home, you can find information on their website or simply call or email the hotel and try to ask.

Per Jones Lang LaSalle (2015), in mature markets in the USA, nearly 50% of full-service hotel stocks are owned by private equity funds, real estate investment trusts (REITs), and institutional investors. The other half is likely in the hands of individuals and families. Some of the top institutional hotel owners are Accor Worldwide, The Blackstone Group, Westmont Hospitality Group, Host Hotels & Resorts, LQ Management, J.E. Robert Cos., ING Clarion Partners, Ashford Hospitality Trust, FelCor Lodging Trust, RLJ Development, Sunstone Hotel Investors, Hersha Hospitality Trust, Strategic Hotels & Resorts, LaSalle Hotel Properties, Loews Hotels and more.

Most of the REITs' value per key and implied leverage ratios are below:

Public REIT Valuations					
Company	Share Price 10/31/22	Enterprise Value per Key[1]	Net Debt per Key[2]	Implied Leverage[3]	Implied Cap Rate[4]
Apple Hospitality REIT	$17.12	$185,271	$50,303	27.2%	6.8%
Ashford Hospitality Trust	$8.12	$167,268	$156,268	93.4%	5.9%
Braemar Hotels and Resorts	$4.93	$397,162	$297,756	75.0%	9.7%
Chatham Lodging Trust	$12.97	$209,205	$100,126	47.9%	6.7%
DiamondRock Hospitality	$9.34	$341,823	$130,472	38.2%	7.1%
Hersha Hospitality Trust	$9.15	$300,533	$197,198	65.6%	7.9%
Host Hotels & Resorts	$18.88	$410,614	$86,638	21.1%	7.9%
Park Hotels & Resorts	$13.08	$234,831	$136,501	58.1%	7.8%
Pebblebrook Hotel Trust	$16.04	$405,953	$175,497	43.2%	6.2%
RLJ Lodging Trust	$12.17	$193,256	$82,909	42.9%	7.7%
Summit Hospitality Group	$8.64	$195,926	$86,483	44.1%	7.1%
Sunstone Hotel Investors	$11.15	$434,375	$91,767	21.1%	6.9%
Xenia Hospitality Group	$17.08	$329,712	$124,713	37.8%	6.9%

Sources: hotelAVE, JF Capital Advisors 10/31/22
[1] Enterprise Value/Key = (Market Cap+Net Debt)/Keys;
[2] Net Debt/Key = Net Debt/Keys;
[3] Implied Leverage = Net Debt/Enterprise Value;
[4] Implied Cap Rate = EBITDA/Enterprise Value

Another interesting list of owners and developers in 2020 is below per the website HotelBusiness.com:

	Company	Location	2020 (as of 6/30) Rooms	2020 (as of 6/30) Hotels	2019 Rooms	2019 Hotels	Leading Brand Affiliates
1	Service Properties Trust	Newton, MA	51,404	1,138	51,349	1,145	Marriott, IHG, Sonesta
2.	Apple Hospitality REIT Inc.	Richmond, VA	29,759	233	29,870	233	Hilton, Marriott, Hyatt
3.	Atrium Hospitality	Alpharetta, GA	22,209	85	22,209	85	Hilton, Marriott, IHG
4.	MCR	New York, NY	13,018	95	12,458	91	Marriott, Hilton
5.	Procaccianti Companies	Cranston, RI	13,002	59	12,637	49	Marriott, Hilton, IHG
6.	Baywood Hotels	Columbia, MD	12,011	116	11,413	111	Hilton, Marriott, IHG
7.	Stonebridge Companies	Denver, CO	10,915	64	10,749	63	Marriott, Hilton, Hyatt
8.	Rockbridge	Columbus, OH	10,627	47	10,627	47	Hilton, Marriott, Hyatt
9.	Kinseth Hospitality Corp	North Liberty, IA	9,951	88	9,860	87	Marriott, Hilton, IHG
10.	Shamin Hotels Inc.	Chester, VA	8,574	62	8,219	59	Hilton, Marriott, IHG
11.	Clarion Partners LLC	New York, NY	8,471	55	8,471	55	Marriott, Hilton
12.	Concord Hospitality Enterprises Company Affiliate	Raleigh, NC	8,015	51	7,263	46	Marriott, Hilton, Hyatt
13	Peachtree Hotel Group	Atlanta, GA	7,824	61	7,824	61	Hilton, Marriott, IHG
14.	HVMG	Atlanta, GA	7,773	47	7,141	42	Hilton, Marriott, Hyatt
15.	Rosen Hotels & Resorts	Orlando, FL	6,694	8	6,694	8	n/a
16.	Commonwealth Hotels LLC	Covington, KY	5,381	44	5,319	44	Hilton, Marriott, Hyatt
17.	InterMountain Management	Monroe, LA	5,346	48	4,727	43	Marriott, Hilton, Hyatt
18.	Waramaug Hospitality	Boca Raton, FL	4,899	39	4,521	37	Marriott, IHG, Hilton
19.	Noble Investment Group	Atlanta, GA	4,434	27	5,364	30	Marriott, Hilton, Hyatt
20.	First Hospitality	Rosemont, IL	4,304	26	4,288	25	Marriott, Hilton, IHG
21.	OTO Development	Spartanburg, SC	4,232	26	4,069	25	Hilton, Marriott, Hyatt
22.	Meyer Jabara Hotels	Danbury, CT	4,126	30	3,929	28	Marriott, Hilton, Hyatt
23.	Arbor Lodging	Chicago, IL	4,038	34	2,358	21	Hilton, Marriott, IHG
24.	Stanford Hotels Corporation	San Francisco, CA	4,004	13	4,004	13	Hilton, Marriott
25.	SREE Hotels LLC	Charlotte, NC	3,463	26	3,463	26	Marriott, Hilton, IHG
26.	GF Hotels & Resorts	Philadelphia, PA	3,457	18	3,457	18	Marriott, Hilton, IHG
27.	Sandpiper Lodging Trust	Richmond, VA	3,410	28	3,161	26	Choice, IHG, Marriott
28.	Giri Hotels	Quincy, MA	3,409	36	3,259	34	Choice, Marriott, Hilton
29.	North Central Group	Middleton, WI	3,365	25	3,197	24	G6 Hospitality, Marriott
30.	CN Hotels	Greensboro, NC	3,238	31	2,648	25	Hilton, Marriott, IHG
31.	Amerilodge Group	Bloomfield Hills, MI	3,213	35	2,633	28	IHG, Marriott, Choice
32.	Chartres Lodging Group	San Francisco, CA	3,016	4	3,301	6	Hilton, Hyatt, Marriott
33.	McKibbon Hospitality	Tampa, FL	2,977	21	2,977	21	Marriott, Hilton, Hyatt
34.	United Capital Corp	Great Neck, NY	2,900	11	2,900	11	Hilton, Marriott
35.	HRI Lodging	New Orleans, LA	2,787	15	2,787	15	Hilton, Hyatt, Marriott
36.	Innisfree Hotels Inc	Gulf Breeze, FL	2,764	19	2,764	19	Hilton, IHG, Marriott
37.	Lowe	Los Angeles, CA	2,718	6	2,855	6	n/a

The Asian American Hotel Owners Association (AAHOA) is the largest hotel owner association in the U.S. The nearly 20,000 AAHOA members own 60 percent of the hotels in the United States (more than 34,000 hotels). AAHOA Members are responsible for 1.7 percent of the nation's GDP. 32% of AAHOA members own independent properties, 82% own branded properties. Plus, 47% of upper-upscale and 41% of luxury hotel properties in the United States are in the hands of its members.

Hotel Stocks and Investments

Hotel ownership is evolving quickly as this asset type becomes more understood by lenders and the investor community as a way to diversify their portfolios.

An excellent way to learn from and participate in the industry is by studying major hotel stocks. Companies listed need to disclose many parts of their strategies, operations and financials in their annual reports in the USA, known as the publicly available online and extensive 10-K Forms. Studying them carefully is recommended. However, hotel businesses are diversified and can encompass hotel management or real state ownership separately. The famous names well known that have stocks listed and their tickers are:

- Marriott International (MAR)
- Hilton Hotels (HLT)
- Wyndham Hotels & Resorts (WH)
- Choice Hotels International (CHH)
- Hyatt Hotels Corporation (H)
- InterContinental Hotels Group (IHG), and more

But those mostly do not own most of the real estate but have management or franchise agreements and focus on an asset-light strategy has recently been their focus. There are also several large hotel management companies that are private without listed stocks.

On the other hand, there are companies that own real estate and focus on hospitality buildings, construction, acquisitions and other hospitality real estate developments, such as:

- Host Hotels & Resorts
- Hersha Hospitality Trust
- Xenia Hotels & Resorts
- Sunstone Hotel Investors
- Pebblebrook Hotel Trust
- Strategic Hotels
- Apple Hospitality, and more

These companies usually hire brands to manage their properties and are organized as Hotel REITs or real estate investment trusts, a way to allow smaller investors to invest in real estate with liquidity. REITs are known to offer high-yield dividends since they are legally required to pay out 90% of taxable income to shareholders. REITs' publicly available financial statements offer an extraordinary source of useful information related to hotels. There are also timeshare or vacation ownership stocks and their financial information that are very interesting too. These companies have primarily split from their major hotel operators and engaged in complex special agreements with these major hotel operators to use their brands. Now they are independent companies named Marriott Vacation Ownership, Wyndham Destinations and Hilton Grand Vacations and others.

Hospitality companies historically are not very profitable when compared to other industries and their margins are difficult to understand due to building depreciation and other accounting rules. However, studying their lengthy 10-K forms can bring valuable insights into the industry to understand what impacts their profitability.

To finance their development, Hotel REITs tend to be leveraged, which means they have a higher proportion of debt than equity. Debt can be beneficial since their interest payments reduce businesses' taxable income and can lead to fewer disbursements (of tax payments) compared to what businesses pay in debt interest.

Also, depreciation, which is high in hotel real estate compared to other industries, reduces the taxable income, and many times companies that appear not profitable are actually offering good returns. Another important data to look at when comparing Hotel REITs is their Price/FFO funds from operations.

Hotel Agency Costs or Conflicts of Interest Between Owners and Management

The divergence of objectives between owners/shareholders and managers, caused naturally by the separation of ownership and control in organizations, has always caused losses to societies, with legal actions, public spending of regulatory agencies, resignations, and deterioration of work relationships. As bigger the companies, the bigger tends to be the separation between ownership and control/management. The costs associated with reducing these conflicts are known as Agency Costs, such as auditing costs, implementation of ethic codes of conduct, segregation of duties to avoid too much decision power in the hands of few managers, and other costs.

Managers can be inclined to try to increase their influence, compensation and job security using the owner's resources. They can also be inclined to not reduce all kinds of waste and avoid taking risks to not generate negative results that could negatively affect their credibility, sometimes missing opportunities. They also can manipulate the financial statements to maximize their bonuses and the market value of the companies they manage on behalf of their owners.

Corporate Governance is an attitude, set of procedures and practices, along with the mindset offered by the controlling managers to owners, that, through the offer of disclosure, compliance, accountability, and fairness good anticipatory practices, tries to reduce these natural conflicts and costs.

These situations described above are applicable to most companies and industries and they also apply to hospitality businesses. In many cases, the agreement between the two parties will stipulate that the general manager or hotel management company takes responsibility for the day-to-day operations while the hotel owner surrenders control and takes a backseat. Generally, the management will be given financial incentives from the owners to keep the business profitable and even to grow the business. With that being said, there can be disputes between owners and the management they use, and there are times when the priorities of management may not necessarily align perfectly with the owner's priorities. Therefore, hotel owners need to choose management carefully and negotiate decision-making powers. It is recommended to offer stock options or even grant stock ownership to managers of maybe up to 15 to 20% to encourage them to act in the owner's best interests.

Financial fraud can occur in many ways inside hotels and depending on their "materiality", they are not even disclosed to owners. Assessing their risks is mostly the responsibility of the hotel controller and the complexity of auditing their practices is high. Just to mention a few examples of significant risks are the risk of not reporting the totality of the revenues, over-discounting, recording expenses not related to the business or from overpriced invoices and inflated payroll.

However, owners and shareholders need to be careful not to over-pressure valuable managers that are naturally good stewards. Excessive controls can be expensive in many ways and sometimes are not necessary. Showing trust but limiting and communicating boundaries can have a very good impact on the longevity and even transformation of managers. The

Stewardship theory defends that most managers, left on their own, can and will act as responsible stewards of the assets they control. Stewardship theorists assume that given a choice between self-serving behavior and pro-organizational behavior, a steward will place a higher value on cooperation.

Hotel Asset Management Roles and Importance

The role of hospitality asset managers should become increasingly important with the growth of the industry and more separation between ownership and management. Many times, a different set of eyes not directly involved with the day-to-day operations is essential to see needs and solutions that might not be visible to the operations teams or owners. Many hotel owners also do not have the knowledge or time to manage their assets properly as hospitality becomes more and more competitive and complex.

No matter the size of the hotel or portfolio of hotels, the asset manager can be very beneficial to owners and management teams alike, where the asset manager brings more knowledge, bridge to help offset agency conflicts and release ownership from many responsibilities. They report to owners but should build more rapport with the operations team, even defending them from the owners on some occasions.

With the increase of corporations, funds and institutions owning hotels that do not know much about hotel businesses, the role of asset managers is becoming more and more important to offset the power hotel management companies have.

Many general managers might not see positively the constant presence and interference of asset managers representing ownership interests, however, with the workload normal to the hotel's operation teams, general managers should welcome the collaborative participation of asset managers if they are knowledgeable and sensitive to timing.

The asset managers serve as consultants remotely and/or presently, providing asset oversight, setting up and monitoring performance levels, goals, updating competitive set data and helping general managers with many tasks, such as finishing financial reports, obtaining financing with banks and investors, defining the best hotel management to hire or to be independent, define systems to use, defining and applying the positioning and marketing strategy, renovations management, successions and more.

It is also important to provide feedback to the general manager on how s/he needs to stretch her/his natural abilities to cover areas that are needed too and send a clear message to the staff that one area is not more important than others. The fact the general manager normally focusses more on certain areas due to her/his natural abilities does not mean that those areas are priorities to the business, as they can wrongly appear in the eyes of the staff.

Asset managers or their trustees should also taste their products and services as occult mystery shoppers since they are less recognized by the staff when compared to the general manager. Be guests in their entire journey, from booking, seeing the property from outside, finding parking, staying in the most remote rooms of the hotel, observing all the minimal details in the rooms, using all the amenities, staying in the lines, see things from different angles, bringing kids, smelling, listening, talking to the staff about their work conditions as a customer, calling departments as a customer, etc. making a routine of those and reporting changes needed are desired practices, on top of following up on them.

The remuneration of the asset manager depends on how much time is spent per hotel and should be linked to the performance of the property. Plus, the owners need to know how to audit the results. The compensation can be expensive if the frequency of engagement is high and many owners might not want to incur such disbursements, deciding to do it themselves or delegate to their general managers. It can be difficult to distinguish or separate the responsibilities of the asset managers and the general managers, such as increasing revenue per available room (RevPAR), etc. Another recommended option is to give asset managers partial ownership in exchange. Sometimes asset managers can also be compensated by evaluating and selling the business under excellent terms, acting like real estate brokers.

There are some firms that offer hotel asset management services or individual consultants, some associated with the Hospitality Asset Managers Association (HAMA), or smaller companies that can help hotel owners. Many professionals come from prior general manager roles, developers from large hotel management companies, Hotel REITs, Big 4s financial service firms and more.

Hotel Chains vs. Independent Hotels and Franchise vs. Management Agreements

Several sources roughly indicate that in 2000 and after, only 25% of European hotels were affiliated with a chain of hotels, but in the United States, this percentage was 70%. Why is the number of independent hotels much higher in Europe than in the USA? Per other sources, in the USA in 2000 and after, roughly occupancy in independent hotels was very similar to the occupancy in chain hotels.

More recent data from 2021 worldatlas.com indicates the top hotel chains worldwide, regardless of the agreement types or flags. Numbers are approximately and constantly changing in bulk from mergers and acquisitions:

1.   Wyndham Hotel & Resorts - 8,941 properties
2.   Marriott International - 7,662 properties
3.   Choice Hotels International - 7,111 properties
4.   Hilton - 6,619 properties
5.   IHG Hotels & Resorts - 5,959 properties
6.   Best Western Hotels & Resorts - 4,037 properties
7.   Radisson Hotel Group - 1,615 properties

Also, below is the list of the biggest *motel* chains worldwide, with approximate figures just for reference:

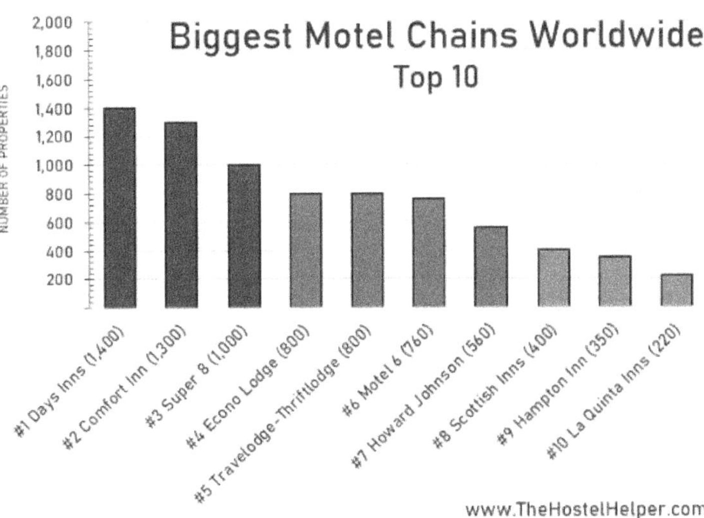

Likely, three-quarters of hotels in the United States are franchises. Between being affiliated with a chain via a franchise agreement or a broader management agreement, the differences are many. In franchise agreements, what is typically offered are:

- the right to use the brand
- the use of their reservation systems
- their revenue management guidance
- their points/rewards/loyalty program
- their procurement deals,

In management agreements, on top of all the above, hotel owners also obtain from the chain:

- full personnel management
- full sales management
- accounting management, and other services

The management of personnel, sales and accounting are among by far the most demanding.

Hotel chains act differently with franchise agreements, where they are only concerned about revenues. In management agreements, they are also concerned with most expenses under their control because it affects their remuneration. The approximate costs to be associated and affiliated with a hotel chain are listed below:

<u>Franchise Agreements</u>
Initial Fee: $40k-$100k
Royalty Fee: 4-7.5% of room sales | Management Fee: $0
System Expenses*: 5-7% of room sales
Total: 9-14.5% of room sales

<u>Management Contracts</u>
Initial Fee: $0
Royalty Fee: 0% | Management Fee: 1.5-3% of gross revenue plus 5-10% of gross operating profit
System Expenses*: 1.5-5% of gross revenue
Total: 3-8% of gross revenue plus 5-10% of gross operating profit

*System Expenses include marketing and advertising, reservations, accounting, purchasing, and training.

Just keep in mind that room sales and gross revenues above, usually are before deductions of OTA commissions.

Per the Business Travel News, Survey of Hotel Companies, the quantity and percentage of property ownership and management structures for the major global brands are below, which shows the higher percentage of franchise agreements compared to management agreements and an increasing trend for asset-light strategies from the part of the operator brands, with very few properties owned. Latest data found is only from the year 2006:

	Franchises Properties	%	Management Contracts Properties	%	Majority Owned Properties	%	Total Properties
InterContinental Hotels	3,204	86%	512	14%	25	1%	3,741
Marriott International	1,783	66%	927	34%	12	0%	2,722
Hilton Hotels Corp.	2,234	82%	397	15%	100	4%	2,731
Accor	1,348	30%	1,881	42%	1,233	28%	4,462
Global Hyatt	245	44%	188	34%	125	22%	558
Wyndham Hotel Group	6,441	100%	32	0%	0	0%	6,473
Carlson Hotels & Resorts	901	96%	17	2%	23	2%	941
Starwood Hotels & Resorts	369	43%	416	48%	83	10%	868
Choice Hotels International	4,208	100%	0	0%	3	0%	4,211
Totals	20,733	78%	4,370	16%	1,604	6%	26,707

Management companies generally do not want owners to interfere. They tend to strive for total managerial control because hotel operations are their area of expertise and the reason they have been hired. Per Hodari, D., Turner, M.J., Sturman, M.C., and Nath, D (2018). The role of hotel owners across different management and agency structures published in the *International Journal of Hospitality and Tourism Administration,* the general managers from both independent and managed hotels acknowledged that their owners influence only financial decisions to a greater extent than operational ones.

The results also revealed that owners involve themselves in properties with hotel management agreements to the same degree they do in independent hotels, with 50 percent of GMs noting that such owners have a moderate to strong influence on the hotel's financial *and* operational decisions. In other words, the hotel management agreement does not seem to reduce an owner's role compared to that of the independent hotels, which do not have contractual restrictions on their involvement. The general managers also reported greater autonomy in hotels that were not overseen by an asset manager.

Many hotels have flags under a franchise agreement but are managed by several other hospitality company names not broadly known by the public. According to a special report from hotelmanagement.net in 2020, these are the top:

2020 rank	Company name	Guestrooms third-party managed in the U.S.	Properties third-party managed in the U.S.
1	Aimbridge Hospitality	164,512	1,170
2	Highgate	42,000	156
3	Crescent Hotels & Resorts	29,572	97
4	HEI Hotels & Resorts	24,852	82
5	Pyramid Hotel Group	19,676	80
6	Concord Hospitality Enterprises	19,048	125
7	HHM	19,000	135
8	Crestline Hotels & Resorts	17,606	118
9	Remington Hotels	17,210	89
10	Hotel Equities	14,658	138
11	TPG Hotels & Resorts	14,625	54
12	Nationwide Hotel Management Company	14,609	122
13	Real Hospitality Group	14,489	109
14	Davidson Hotels & Resorts	14,084	47
15	Dimension Development Company	12,677	67

Per the American Hotel and Lodging Association (AH&LA), Directory of Hotel & Lodging Companies published annually, in addition to brand operators, there are more than 800 independently managing companies globally, managing approximately 12,000 properties, some of which of course also manage branded franchised properties.

Turning Around Underperforming Hotels

What is an underperforming hotel? It depends. It can be a hotel that is not delivering the profitability owners would like to or simply a hotel that is not satisfying guests or their employees.

I prefer to define an underperforming hotel the one that is not reaching its full potential in several aspects, reflected in the key performance indicators (KPIs) such as:

- Online Reviews
- Occupancy
- Average Daily Rates
- RevPAR
- INDEXES compared to a carefully selected Competitive Set

Other financial indicators are worth analyzing, based on a defined timeframe for comparisons, such as:

- Debt Leverage Ratios
- Current Liquidity
- Labor Costs per Room

The issue is that identifying full potential requires a strategic outside-the-box view, acumen, and experience to see the possibilities and repositioning many do not.

To properly position a hotel, it demands a constant reassessment of the environment it is in, such as its city or location, well-defined competitive set, customers' demographic shifts, nearby businesses and attractions, staffing trends and more. The repositioning of the hotel is usually much slower and ideally needs to be anticipatory, which is risky. The costs of being proactive might be higher than reactive, but if properly done, it can pay off for a long time, reaching a more sustainable competitive advantage.

There are many hotels that can apparently look to be underperforming, but in reality, they are extremely profitable. Or vice versa, there are hotels that look astonishing and trendy, with the latest modern or luxurious furniture and facilities, but constantly only generate financial losses to their owners or lenders.

Financial profitability is one of the main indicators of success, however, it is not the only one depending on the owner's interests, and success can be measured by other means such as the high service that is delivered to their customers, the satisfaction of its employees or the benefits the hotel offers to the community.

It is not easy to turn underperforming hotels around it, especially if there is no support from ownership. Owners will have to have an open mindset mentality and allow the team to test and take risks. Many times owners already have a rigid outdated vision, lack financial capabilities, are satisfied, or don't know how to improve.

Usually, changes are implemented most of the time by new owners that risk purchasing the property believing it was not reaching its full potential or by new general managers that come with a different experience, new mindset and energy. Rarely exterior consultants or asset managers are engaged unless the size of the hotel is large. Active owners might try to turn their properties around before requesting help. The help can come in the form of obtaining better financing to pave the owner's visions.

Feedback also can come from customers via verbal or formalized reviews and from the team members, however, from my experience, the feedback from those stakeholders usually doesn't lead to disruptive changes, unfortunately. Management needs to find better ways to obtain and assess feedback from its stakeholders.

Adaptive improvements are always necessary and should be constant. It can be in many areas such as on the facilities, replacing certain staff, compensating, and giving autonomy to the staff, creative service, cleanliness, safety, attracting different segmentation of customers and other examples go on and on. However, many times changes are not needed, and hotels need to be careful not to change in a way that will put at risk its longevity.

There is a fascinating aspect of old hotels older than 40 years that are performing well. Usually, they went through one or two full-scope renovation cycles and deciding how to renovate an older property without losing its characteristics but still bringing proper updates is a great skill that will be demanded more as hotels get older and older. When staying in older properties that are thriving, we can also see the results of implemented best operations through the physical structure, marketing positioning and staff.

Deflagging Hotels

Hotel developers and owners use franchises to have a sense of revenue security relying on perceived brand recognition, have access to specific distribution channels, bulk negotiation power, and established loyalty programs with the intent to garner higher returns in markets they believe prefer branded hotels. In exchange for all this, stakeholders pay fees to the brand, commonly 5 to 15% of all their revenue.

Younger travelers though, are behaving in a way that shows they have more brand loyalty directly to online travel agencies or metasearches like TripAdvisor, Booking.com, Expedia, Agoda, Trip.com, Google Hotels, Hostelworld and Airbnb, rather than legacy hotel brands despite their efforts to cater to this segment. Upcoming younger generations aren't as brand loyal to the large hotel chains as previous generations. Travelers who book hotel rooms on mobile devices prefer online travel agencies to hotel brand sites by a three-to-one margin. Additionally, online travel agencies are usually preferred over booking directly with hotels because of better price transparency and comparisons.

Travelers' preferences are changing, and many don't want cookie-cutter hotels anymore. Usually, they want an experience that is unique and different, which big-brand hotels can't always provide. That is partially due to the absence of owners' personal touches and, of course, brand standards that do not permit such modifications. Some hotels have taken note of this, and they've adapted by making their businesses more *boutique*.

Marriott has 20+ hotel brands and below is approximately the number of hotels "deflagged" among all brands according to information found online at *marriott.gcs-web.com/static-files/8e7ae9df-c5f7-4bcf-8727-674e86a748ec*. Apparently, a rising trend. Note that Marriott's portfolio grew considerably with the Starwood's merger in 2016 and that the data below likely also include hotels deflagged due to Covid-19 in 2020 and 2021:

Year	2013	2014	2015	2016	2017	2018	2019	2020	2021
Deflagged Hotels	121	115	117	87	176	266	156	213	561*

*In 2021 alone, there were 137 Residence Inns and 201 Courtyards deflagged, totaling almost 50,000 rooms

While this is set to increase, like the number of specialized hotels, inns and bed and breakfasts, or boutique and independent hotels, there will still be too many choices for the typical traveler, causing them to choose based likely on price.

It is predicted that hospitality businesses that provide a unique experience and *are cheaper* than their competition will greatly benefit. And this trend is relevant, per Nathan Mayfield in a Forbes article from 2021.

Being independent has its benefits and drawbacks as next:

- Agility - Independent hotels hold another unique opportunity compared to flagged properties, the flexibility to quickly reposition themselves without the red tape of multi-level decision-making. Moving away from corporate brand affiliations can mean hassle-free and streamlined protocols.

- Pricing - Deflagged hotels can change pricing strategies, add or remove services, and make purchasing decisions to better their performance as they see fit.

- Targeting: furthermore, young traveler segments (Millennials and Gen-Zers) are growing, and it is becoming more relevant for hotels to appeal to them. They prioritize selecting a property based on unique amenities, culture, sustainability, digital touchpoints, and price. As an independent hotelier, a deflagged hotel can develop customized programming to capture these customers with ease.

- Marketing Fees – not participating in the brand marketing program, which is very generic and broad, other investments should be expected, including but not limited to the need to hire more staff, increase individual marketing spending, upgrade technology and distribution systems, improve internal practices and procedures, and define a unique and memorable brand experience.

- Staffing – unflagging means that it will stop access to multi-level infrastructure, including support across a variety of staffing levels, from senior executive level leadership to administrative support. Along with the resources to staff efficiently, flagged hotels further provide standard operating procedures, developed from years of on-the-ground experience, backed by a proven track record of success. Expect higher costs to obtain any other type of assistance on your own.

Per Eyster and deRoos, in their 2009 book The Negotiation and Administration of Hotel Management Contracts, owners can generally terminate the contract with a branded operator only if they can prove gross negligence, fraud, or misrepresentation on the part of operator, or on the event of bankruptcy, insolvency, merger, or corporate reorganization of the operator. In operator agreements, termination clauses due to poor operator performance are becoming increasingly present. There are many details to it, but the basic revolves around the need to maintain a minimum cash flow before fixed charges and debt service, and minimum RevPAR indexes levels.

And then there is the technology. How will the newly independent hotel operate without the brand's existing technology stack? A hotel requires a suite of sophisticated tools to manage reservations, deploy housekeepers, track maintenance, distribute inventory and accomplish a variety of other tasks.

The process of deflagging, or removing a brand or chain from properties is a very difficult, risky and complex process. However, for hotels that want to go solo, it has become easier than ever to find software, workers and companies that support independent operations nowadays with skilled, robust but easy-to-use, and affordable options like:

- Cloud-Based Property Management Systems (PMS)
- Integrated Channel Management Systems
- Automated Integrated Revenue Management Systems
- Automatic Payment Processing
- Affordable Door Lockset Systems
- Easier Online Marketing and Reporting
- Brand Creators
- Website Developers
- Several Affordable Global Freelancers
- Streamlined Supplier Deliveries from Amazon, Walmart, etc.
- Online Accounting and Payroll
- Cloud Computing Storage
- Streamlined OTA Channel Extranets and more

For creative-minded hoteliers, the ability to craft a unique experience on their own terms is one of the principal benefits of being independent. The focus on a better guest experience likely will result in better online reviews. Also, Thomas Goodwin of Fillmore Hospitality says, *"the big challenge for independents has been building credibility and consumer confidence. As hotel reviews have become transparent, the whole world has changed. The democratization of reviews is the best thing that has ever happened to great hotel operators."*

Without a clear niche, it can be challenging to thrive as an independent hotel. The landscape is simply so saturated and competitive, with consumers focusing less on brand and more on price, location, and quality of experience.

Demand for unique, independent hotels and experiences is well known by groups like Preferred Hotels & Resorts, which has welcomed several new independent hotel members to their portfolio that were once hard brands or part of other collections. Consider these three hotels that are now part of Preferred Hotels & Resorts: The Trump SoHo, in Manhattan, was recently reborn as The Dominick; Le Richemond, in Geneva, Switzerland, jettisoned the Dorchester Collection; and The DeSoto in Savannah, Ga., used to fly the Hilton flag.

These moves, Philipp Weghmann, EVP of Europe for Preferred, said, are a sign of the growing strength and acceptance of independent hotels by the traveling public, and their appeal to owners. This is strikingly evident in the luxury space, where there has been a growing momentum of hotels deflagging and joining collections such as Preferred, which lends sales, marketing and distribution services to more than 650 global hotels. More examples of this include the former Ritz-Carlton, Palm Beach, which became the Eau Palm Beach several years ago; the Pulitzer Amsterdam, which left the Luxury Collection; The Stafford London was with Kempinski for several years; and the Hotel Metropole in Geneva was a Swissotel for about a decade. All of these properties are now members of Preferred. *"The list goes on and on and on"* Weghmann said.

While companies like Marriott and Hilton are still relatively new to it, with their Autograph and Curio collections, respectively. (Both Marriott and Hilton now have more than one collection brand in their portfolios.) Weghmann doesn't pull any punches. *"It means good times for us because we've been in the space for much longer than other collections, so we're a lot better-equipped to service these hotels then a Marriott or a Hilton, or the other hard brands with their relatively new collections for independent hotels."*

Weghmann has seen a "huge appetite" from both owners and developers to go independent in recent years, a trend that he credits to several factors. "One is that they have realized that being with a hard brand does not necessarily guarantee superior performance anymore," he said, citing studies from companies like HVS and Horwath HTL, which have found strong occupancy and rates at independent properties. "Many times, it's actually the independent hotel that will perform better in RevPAR in a certain market than the flagged property," he said.

While the revenue may not be higher than a branded hotel, Weghmann said, the costs can be another factor that can lead investors' appetites for independent hotels. Franchise fees at a branded hotel can vary between 6 percent and 10 percent of revenue, Weghmann estimated, and higher for a management contract. *"With Preferred, the cost is usually 1 to 3 percent of all rooms revenue, which is a very attractive proposition for a lot of owners"* he said. Lowering the membership fee allows the hotel's revenue to *"flow through to the bottom line"* he added.

Another factor is contract duration, which also provides more flexibility for owners. Preferred's contracts are typically around five years, which can be well lower than what hard brands contract. Weghmann argued also that being tied down to a hard brand's contract "encumbers" an asset, which can have an onerous impact on the sale of the hotel in the future.

Most of the hotels that drop their brands to join an independent collection are in primary and secondary cities, as well as some resorts. *"As you go into tertiary cities and very remote resort destinations, there may be more of an advantage to be with a hard brand because they may potentially be able to help you market the destination a little bit more aggressively"* Weghmann acknowledged. *"But in a lot of places, the independent hotel is really what the traveler is looking for and, therefore, as a hotel owner, you also want to be proposing that, rather than, proposing a cookie-cutter hotel."*

If chains are not attracting independent-minded millennials, they are at least attracting lenders, who see a recognizable name as an added security for their investment. *"The banks traditionally have viewed the hard brands as a guarantee for solid performance, and that made it a little harder for hotel developers to go with a soft brand,"* Weghmann said. *"That has changed, and there's enough information, enough studies out there now that show the strong performance of independent hotels."* As such, the banks and the lending community at large are getting more and more comfortable with soft brands. *"You will continue to see this shift that is already taking place both for new-builds, new properties that start out as an independent right from the beginning, and obviously hotels that may start with a flag for a few years and then deflag when they think the time is right"* Weghmann adds.

According to a survey conducted on HotelierMiddleEast.com, 38% felt that owners look to deflag as they want to maximize their profit, while 25% put it down to souring relations between owners and operators over Key Performance Indicators (KPIs). 19% felt that operators didn't achieve the desired revenues.

"The new trend is that hotel owners sign an agreement with international or regional hotel operators for anywhere between 20 to 60 years. By the terms of the agreement, the conditions are one-sided where the owners are sometimes trapped by the brand and legally cannot terminate this agreement for the duration of the contract. The owner has no say in the hotel and the operator becomes like an owner of the property without paying for it".

Performance tests are one of the first logical areas to look at when an owner is considering terminating its relationship with an operator. While performance tests seem appealing by title, in reality, most performance tests are very difficult to fail.

This is because performance tests are usually formed of two parts, one tied to budgeted gross operating profit and another tied to revenue per available room compared to a set of competitive hotels, and failure of the test must be in a number of consecutive years.

Further hindered by cure rights, these tests are effectively moving targets and tests are likely to not be applicable if there was a force majeure event in the market. There are, however, sometimes better-negotiated performance tests that are of substance, and these may provide recourse to an owner in a way that more standard tests do not.

In the case of management agreements, owners need to consider that any rebranding exercise will need to give special consideration to the hotel employees in the hotel, and strategies should be adopted to motivate and retain this core element of the hotel operations to ensure a smooth transition. The legal employment contract must also be carefully considered. It is more often the case in the region that employees are sponsored by the owner, but key employees might sometimes be on secondment from the operator being required to move from one property to another. The continuity of employees is an important consideration in achieving continuity of operations.

Hotel owners that decide to go independent will also need to begin talks with their lenders to agree to the appointment of alternative operators. Complex and disruptive outcomes can arise if the lenders are not on board and actively engaged in any rebranding process. Additionally, the existence of signed non-disturbance agreements between the operators and banks, where the banks cannot disturb property occupants in the event of a foreclosure, might add additional layers of complications that need careful consideration.

Hotel Brands will have to become more flexible with their compensation structures, invest their own capital in partnerships, share more risks, loose standards, and innovatively position themselves if they want to continue competing since owners who do not want to be held back by stricter and specific rules, with the help of technologies, are increasing in numbers.

Reserve Funds for Renovations and Challenges

Hotels normally spend a lot of resources and money on renovations to replace items that failed prematurely or that reached their maximum useful lives. Note the reserve funds are for the replacement of items, not additions or major upgrades. To be competitive and sustain good rates and reviews, hotels need to keep an updated appearance, replacing items in shorter cycles than normal. Defining how it will be done depends on how the hotel wants to position itself.

Just to give a perspective of a few of the thousands of items that will need replacements are roofs, railings, sidings, windows, doors, door locks, floors, paintings, fixtures, furniture, window covers, televisions, outlets, countertops, sinks, cabinets, bathtubs, toilets, mirrors, lighting, mattresses, linen, pool decks, accessibility equipment, water heaters, piping, air-conditions, appliances, washers, dryers, pool furniture, asphalt, elevators, and more, and that is for many times hundreds of rooms and extensive exterior areas.

These replacements are expensive, and as a good best practice, hotels should reserve funds apart to have enough when those replacements are needed. By properly planning and reserving funds years in advance to perform needed future renovations, many hotels avoid incurring costly loan interests later.

The challenges also are to properly forecast the future needs and costs, plus keep those funds intact from operating expenses. Hotels with few owners tend not to be much loyal to reserves and save such funds, but other hospitality types, such as timeshares, are more organized regarding it since they must follow established regulations and have more power over their many partial owners.

The International Society of Hospitality Consultants (ISHC), in partnership with the Hospitality Asset Managers Association (HAMA), presented a CapEx 2018 study of capital expenditures and repairs and maintenance spending in the hotel industry that highlights the levels of expenditures needed based on several factors such as hotel types, locations and ownership structure from 902 hotels in 139 different markets across the United States.

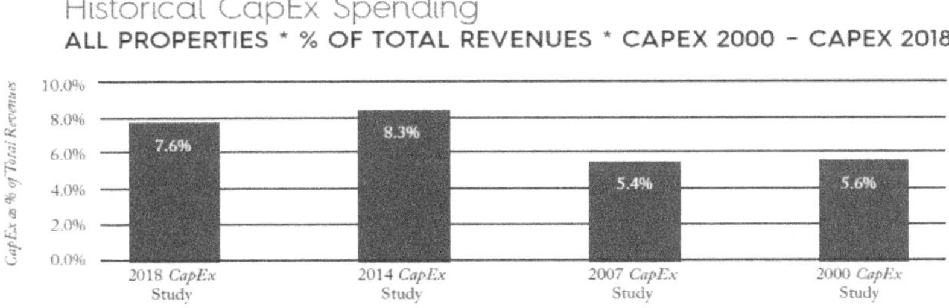

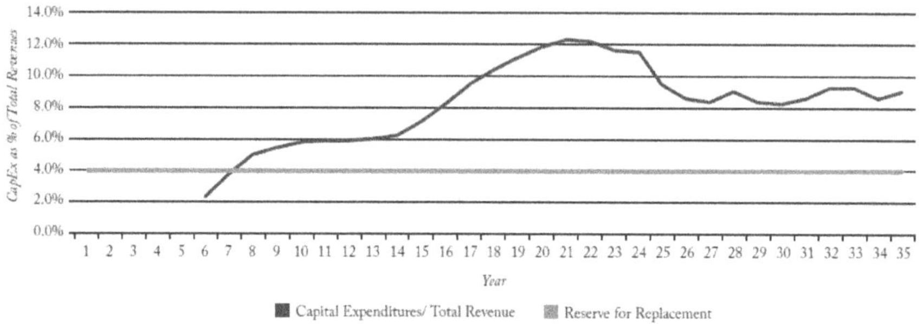

CapEx by Average Daily Rate (ADR)
ALL PROPERTIES * 2013 - 2017

Average Daily Rate	Number of Properties	Average Age	CapEx % of Total Revenues	CapEx Per Available Room Per Year
	2018 CapEx Study	2018 CapEx Study	2018 CapEx Study	2018 CapEx Study
All Properties	902	21.2	7.6%	$4,877
<$100	256	17.5	14.4%	$2,435
$100-$200	496	19.0	8.2%	$3,726
>$200	150	34.8	6.8%	$8,106

In a nutshell, a way to properly define how much to reserve every period is to note all items that will need replacement in the future, usually looking 30 years ahead, forecast how long they will last and how much they will cost when the time comes. Gather all these data and forecast how much will be needed each period to start reserving as much as possible with the help of a spreadsheet or specific software for much larger portfolios. The reserved money can be invested in a low-risk investment, and it is important to note that new items usually should not be purchased with reserve funds, only items that are being replaced.

The challenge of forecasting useful lives with items nowadays of lower quality, plus their future costs in inflationary scenarios is difficult. On top of that, it is not only the cost of the items themselves but also the design, labor to install, discard, shipping and storage that needs to be added to the equation.

Hospitality Jobs Burnout, Turnover and Possible Solutions

There is a general perception that the hospitality industry, among a few others, is comprised of mostly low-level skilled workforce that naturally burns out fast, with shorter lengths of permanency in their jobs, which means high turnover. If this perception is true, when compared to other industries, that causes higher recruiting and training costs. However, we need to be careful in tagging these as being the case and real problems to the industry, sometimes it is a necessary intrinsic characteristic of the industry.

It is also important to distinguish the particularities of lodging accommodation providers and restaurants since they are very different businesses. This material focuses on the lodging accommodation providers.

There are many academic articles focusing on hotel job burnout characteristics and turnover predecessors. It is not easy to find job turnover level statistics and compare them with other industries since data are often kept private. Other service workers such as teachers, nurses, social workers, and health care professionals have been reported to exhibit high job burnout rates (e.g., Acker, 1999; Martin & Schinke, 1998). Hospitality workers also tend to exhibit signs of high burnout rates (Buick & Thomas, 2001; Pienaar & Willemse, 2008).

One of the reasons for higher turnover is that hospitality businesses tend to be in areas where there are similar employment offers, making the decision to change easier. Other reasons are related to the natural challenges of constantly pleasing different types of customers, low pay rates, longer hours, and lack of professional management, among also the personal characteristics of each employee and their demographic and economic status. Management needs to identify acceptable turnover levels and act if they surpass the acceptable levels. Many of the costs of turnover are not easy to measure as well.

As industry insiders, we know that hotel managers tend to spend a great deal of the 24 hours of the day working. The nature of operating a business that needs to function on a twenty-four-hour basis when most of the other businesses are closed is challenging. In hotels, customer demands usually are higher out of business hours when they need to have breakfast, checkout or prepare to go to sleep, plus all that happens in a hotel are most of the times characterized as urgent, such as guests demands, maintenance issues, staff quitting, and including the need to sell the rooms that night. It is a type of business that needs constant and urgent management attention, per Peter Venison in his book. Hotel managers need to prioritize smartly and ideally spend most of their time at the property during those high-demand times, including weekends and holidays. For those that like to have these different schedules and maybe do not need to raise a family of younger kids, it can be quite interesting though.

In terms of solutions and best practices to tackle these apparent problems, offering original customer service can help, which many times *place the interests of hospitality employees first* and leads to a more original and better customer experience. Satisfied and self-confident employees tend to transmit this positive trait to customers. The key here is to keep the staff that naturally can offer it. What is meant by original customer service is that one that *skips* the common behaviors we experience from interacting with staff that was clearly trained to answer situations in standardized ways, using polite and politically correct words we all know can sound fake. The act of faking also generates discomfort for both customers and employees. Originality comes from giving autonomy to the staff to expose their own ways of expressing themselves physically and verbally.

Despite the fast pace of the industry, managers need to be extra careful in recruiting. Identifying desirable personal characteristics and bonds created with management can result in better day-to-day work relationships and lower turnover rates.

Employees' ownership participation experiments can also contribute, despite being rare and difficult to implement. A sense of ownership is valuable, but it can also create conflict and inertia if the skills levels are very different, and each employee has a different vision for the future of the business.

There is a lot of research and literature in the field of human resources and job motivation to reduce turnover from business administration articles, magazines and books that are recommended to be consulted to help tackle this challenge faced by the hospitality industry.

Hospitality jobs overall offer great opportunities to grow, learn, meet new people and travel, with work visa opportunities, probably better than any other industry. If you choose the hospitality industry for your career, it's important to recognize which skills must be honed. Developing your hospitality skills is an ongoing process that requires regular practice and will not happen overnight. However, knowing what you need to improve will lay the groundwork and motivate you to apply it daily. The skills can be self-taught or guided and trained by the company. Equipping ourselves with the right skills not only helps us prevent emotional and physical exhaustion but also enables our business to achieve a higher standard than anyone else, meaning people come to us over the competition. Guests may come for the accommodation and food, but they will stay for the good customer service.

Hospitality jobs are usually divided between the ones with mostly direct physical contact with guests and the ones from the back office, academia, or corporate offices with minimal direct physical contact with guests, but mostly via the phone, email with guests or physical contact with suppliers and co-workers only. The focus of these insights is on the jobs that have direct physical contact with guests, as they are the majority in hospitality. Ultimately, the hospitality industry is about connecting with people, whether that be your customers or co-workers. Of course, skills and experience can be taught and learned, but a good attitude can't, and therefore it is such a critical element for employers to consider.

Usually described as exciting jobs, these can be very demanding on the body and mind. However, many humans prefer not to be confined to an office and prefer the fact every day is different. That is the reason why when hiring, it is important to understand personality traits that have more chances of being suitable to the environment required. Providing enough time for new hires to adapt is also highly recommended. This tentative matchmaking while hiring and on the job is beneficial to the employees and to the company, leading to better day-to-day operations and less turnover.

What personality type is best for working in hospitality? The field is so open and diverse that one "best type" is hard to pin down per Peter Zacchilli and Latie Davin from Johnson & Wales University. According to them, the traits desired are (please read each one of them slowly and self-evaluate):

- Motivated
- Organized
- Flexible
- Empathetic
- Creative Problem-Solver
- Global and Culturally Aware

Other traits found from different sources are:

- Communicative, especially Listener
- Resilient
- Team Worker
- Time Manager
- Self-Starter
- Multi-Tasker
- Adaptative
- Attentive to Details

The resilience trait is quite interesting. If you are new to hospitality, you should know that it is not a career for the thin-skinned. To make it through a shift, you will often have to endure high levels of stress caused by constant multitasking, a lot of running back and forth, and sometimes demanding customers or co-workers. Most of the time, all demands are with a sense of urgency. The good news is that anyone can learn how to remain optimistic, patient and productive despite difficulties.

Thickening your skin is usually a case of experience, but it's also about training your mind. You need to be at peace with any challenges you face and, in fact, use them to improve yourself. You should recognize that a lot of what happens is probably out of your control and you are not responsible for how others behave, only for your actions. This mindset frees the mind and improves productivity. You will spend less time worrying about things you can't control and focus on what you can. Resilience is not only important for making things easier for yourself but also for maintaining a professional image. Customers and colleagues respect those who can remain calm and constructive during adversity.

Despite all, hospitality companies can position themselves differently by bringing employees with different personality traits to differentiate themselves from the competition. Offering authentic customer service and different experiences is a risk that can pay off. Just don't forget to ask for guests' feedback and monitor the online reviews to see if it is working. On certain occasions, these practices and how management fosters these behaviors slowly will also change the type of employees, and guests, your business attracts.

Guest-to-Guest Value Co-Creation Insights in Hospitality

When thinking about hospitality, most of us think about the interactions guests have with the staff. Often, we tend to forget the importance of interactions guests have with other guests, which ultimately affects the image they will have of your business.

In hospitality, more than in any other industry, the interactions among guests positively or negatively are intense and affect how they perceive their experiences, which, even though it is not apparently under our control, affects the impressions they have of your overall hospitality offer.

Customer-to-customer or guest-to-guest interactions are complex, depending on the cultures from the locations where the business is located, how the business designs or promotes it and other factors. In hostels, resorts and cruises, for example, due to the natural closer proximity guests are from one another and the fact most basic needs are attended to, these interactions tend to be even more intense.

People usually identify themselves with others of the same age and social economic status. Cultural differences, gender and other characteristics, besides also being important, are not major in my point of view. Hospitality providers that can attract similar guests tend to harvest better results. Such good atmospheres are observed in universities, music concerts and hostels, that normally attract similar people already based on their demographics, economic power and interests.

According to Maslow in his pyramid of human necessities, the need for socialization and belongingness are in the middle of necessities sought after basic needs are met. The better attendance of the social and belongingness necessities, I believe, *is the next frontier in hospitality*, and some businesses are already exploring it for a while, just started, or are at least trying it. Some examples of these businesses are the resort chain Club Med, the sharing platform Airbnb (despite mostly fostering relationships between hosts, which are hospitality providers, and guests), and most hostels. Airbnb though, despite it started fostering stronger social relationships between hosts and their guests, later shifted and focused mostly in rentals of places without the presence of hosts, which makes the bulk of its revenues.

In facilitating customer-to-customer value co-creation, the hospitality industry can provide more value, even through strategic alliances with technology providers and nearby businesses that do not cost much and are intended to offer tools and spaces to help hotels explore an untapped demand for greater social leisure overall experiences.

Several articles state that, in a global society that is becoming increasingly connected through the wonders of the internet, people are becoming more isolated on a local level, and that applies even to the most extroverts. The sociologist Ray Oldenburg has argued that the missing ingredient is what he coined the "third place", spots beyond home or work where people can truly gather and connect. This loneliness derives from an unfulfilled need for belonging that the internet cannot fulfill. Some hospitality companies, such as Airbnb and hostels, understand this human need and foster communities of customers looking for socialization. Hospitality companies are in a great position, compared to other industries, to help people fulfill what Abraham Maslow (1943) calls 'the human need for a sense of belonging' in his famous pyramid of hierarchy of needs below:

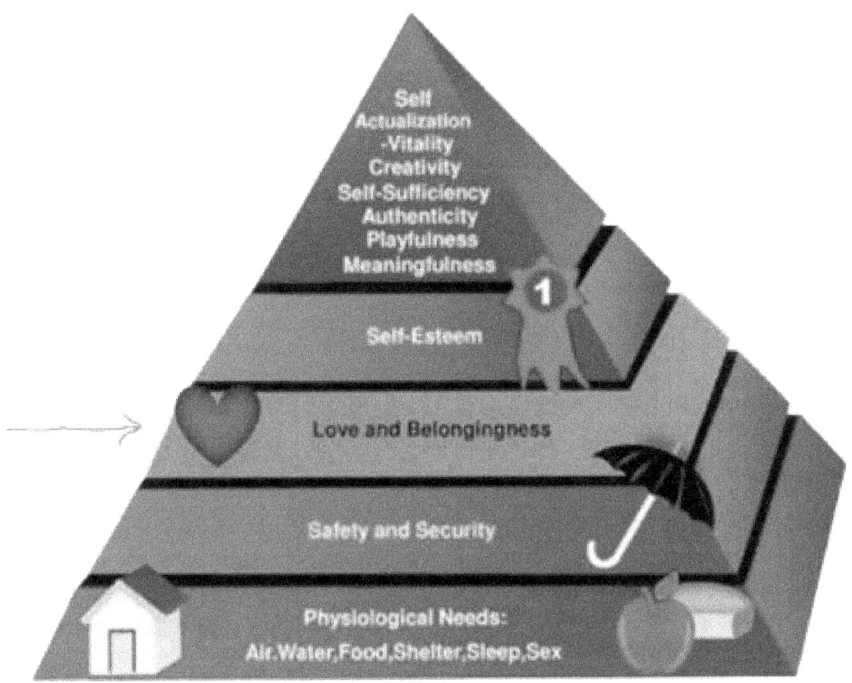

One of the reasons why hospitality is developing at a rapid pace is due to its capability of bringing people together face-to-face and that share common interests. Once facilitating better customer-to-customer interactions, the industry relieves the responsibilities of its employees to be the only providers of great customer service and shares the responsibility of this delivery with other customers in a win-win situation.

However, there is still a lot to explore. Some initiatives, many times, begin through the correct use of technology itself, stimulating personal interactions rather than only online connectivity. Balancing an adequate usage of technology and helping to bring people to environments that avoid their' own technology usage is a way hospitality companies are hoping to solve this recent phenomenon of 'real-world' social isolation. In some studies, this isolation is cited to be a public-health threat even worse than obesity or smoking. Plenty of other social trends are making us feel more untethered than previous generations: people are less religious, marrying later, having fewer kids at older ages, and growing old with no companion.

Large hospitality organizations are also concerned with how technology is going to impact their business, and how there are ways to use it to the advantage of the organization. The most significant takeaway is that the right social interactions are key, and this is what needs to be improved and facilitated to unleash (or recover) what was lost in this human need for socialization.

According to Steverman (2019), not long ago, our community wasn't just a few close friends and family members, or a couple of tolerable co-workers. It was many people who made us feel less lonely on a regular basis. A sense of community was where we went for advice, intel, or gossip. It's where people found people to date and marry, and in a crisis, it brought people together. Most hospitality companies only help fulfill the first two bottom-level needs of physiological and safety. However, others, such as Airbnb and hostels, (and one of the reasons for their success), do not just offer lodging accommodations that were never thought of before, but they also offer a sense of 'building a community' of travelers fulfilling such 'third level human need'. Airbnb, for example, hosts through diversity and inclusion, which is shaping its slogan, "Belong Anywhere."

It is a dilemma though, where businesses try to attract and converge similar people together via their marketing propositions to ease their experiences, but also there is the importance of converging different people together to foster multicultural acceptance, learning and tolerance, that if achieved, leads to strong personal satisfaction. Maybe a combination of both is recommended.

Another problem appears to be that people in contemporary societies are not dedicating, or finding time, to have quality leisure and socializing experiences. Today people spend most of their leisure time watching TV, on their computers and phones, or trying to relax, not physically socializing. A trend of less leisure time dedicated to vacations, especially among North Americans, is tracked by ProjectTimeOff.com, a coalition of organizations intended to increase vacation time. Hospitality companies are at the forefront of delivering this easier than most other industries because they already have the stage set and should take advantage of fulfilling this need meanwhile profiting and helping people at the same time. It is somehow simple but not fully quite there yet.

During my infancy and teen ages, my family went several times to Club Med *villages*, a French chain of resorts that is present all over the world, and they are somehow expensive. In most of those weekend or week-long trips, we were accompanied by a great group of people staying together. Not all vacation groups had that special feeling, but in the groups when we were all connected by common interests and kids and adults were of similar ages, the higher sense of enjoyment offset all struggles in booking, paying higher prices, transporting, etc. Good memories that we all carry with us today.

Those groups were incentivized to form by travel agents or an organizer, and convincing people to join wasn't that difficult of a task once they were informed who had already confirmed or was in the thought of joining. The groups even went above and beyond to share the costs for friends that couldn't pay due to recent financial problems. This sense of community is very special and difficult to find. Altogether, it wasn't easy for the travel agent or organizer to always match personalities, preferences, dates, etc., and I felt better tools should be available for whoever is seeking greater leisure time. In timeshare properties, regular resorts or cruises, guests don't have ways to smartly know or meet who will be or is part of that experience (before, during and after). Most families get isolated because the activities performed are by far not enough or thoughtfully planned and organized. The hospitality industry has a lot still to drink from this fountain of possibilities and already provides most of the structure to make that happen.

Some hotel and resort companies are collecting data on leisure preferences but don't know how to connect the dots or better use this data for the benefit of their consumers. When we socialize, trying to build meaningful long-term connections, it is difficult to find who has similar demographics and also shares other leisure interests our family or we have. Introductory conversations in most of our social gatherings are often limited and superficial. To meet others that will encourage us to have more and greater face-to-face and offline leisure time, there is nothing better than starting by sharing a similar combination of leisure interests. However, this is not as easy as it appears and I believe that even at places we already go for social leisure or are planning to join, it should exist a better way to make the most of it. For these reasons, hotels should work to offer a smarter way to share time and make guests become friends, and that also includes more social spaces.

Finding people by age, gender, combination of leisure interests shared, city they live, school, work, events they are going to, age of children, resorts/cities/cruises they will be or are staying at when traveling and more is a very difficult task. Some have tried to facilitate the process but failed. Facilitating meaningful social interactions altogether can improve the image of your company and increase referrals to outsiders.

The data, when available, can also be used to better shape leisure offers and personalize stays if desired, such as by knowing through easy-to-access top preferred leisure interests of customers, cities they have the desire to go next, how guests are engaging with other members, just to mention a few.

Helping the industry to solve its flaws and improve the value proposition altogether has been a very interesting process. Solving certain issues will even affect how the industry attracts and retains talent. If hospitality companies conclude that there is a demand out there to fulfill better socializing needs and facilitate the discovery of greater leisure friends, plus understand that it is in a great position to deliver it, not by fighting technology but by using it in its favor, great achievement can occur for the industry and even society in general. This can also be a source of competitive advantage to the industry and specific companies that explore it more intensively.

Hotel Environmental, Social and Governance Advancements and Challenges

There are a lot of discussions nowadays on how the hospitality industry can be more sustainable environmentally, socially and economically, and more and more guests want to travel sustainably. For lodging accommodation providers, on the environmental side, hotels, from my point of view, can focus on a few things that cause a higher positive impact.

Hotels' impacts are high on the environmental level, occupying spaces, generating CO2 outputs, spending energy, consuming water and generating waste. The goals then should be to first reduce the impact in a way that does not affect much the guests' experience desired and secondly offset efficiently the impact.

In the day-to-day operations, waste and disposal reduction should be central, focusing on trash, cleaning and laundry disposal. Less frequent, but still more frequent than in other industries, is the disposals from building renovations, when in shorter cycles, hotels need to renovate and change several case and soft goods, such as furniture and everything we can see inside and outside the rooms. Construction materials also generate a lot of waste, and new construction materials in the buildings can be more eco-friendly from sustainable sources; however, those sometimes tend to be more expensive.

Back to the day-to-day disposals, the use of toiletry packages provided to guests, such as soap wraps, large soap bar remainings, shampoos, conditioners and body lotions packages are in high volume and many times made of plastic. Discarding the remaining toilet paper rolls is also common and excessive. The way hospitality companies are replacing that high amount of disposals is by providing reusable larger dispensers or offering less quantity. Regarding laundry, hotels can use eco-friendly products and detergents to reduce the impact of its disposal.

Measures such as proper insulation of roof and walls, energy-efficient lighting such as LED, high-efficiency plumbing fixtures like shower heads, toilets and sinks that reduces flow and smart systems that control air conditioning and lightning when not in need are types of investments that can be high but pays off in the mid and long term.

To save energy, hotels can use smart air conditioning and lighting sensor systems that reduce usage when guests are not in the room. Hotels can do a better job sorting the trash for recycling and ensuring their waste manager provider is disposing it properly. In summary, these are the practices among many that have a strong environmental impact on lodging accommodations.

On the social level, the hospitality industry already employs a huge quantity of employees, however, it is known for not paying much. In the accommodations industry, I believe hotels should make a better effort to pay their staff better. I know labor is usually a big expense in their income statement, but it is important to try to pay employees above market levels due to the many invisible costs that occur if your business does not, such as turnover, hiring, training, etc. On the other hand, it is also important to be properly staffed in terms of quantity of employees because the benefits of having a lot of employees help to create a good environment among themselves and more people to help handle guests. To reduce costs, hotels can hire younger staff members that usually have more energy.

I believe the government should provide more incentives to lodging accommodation providers because hotels often attract revenue from other states and abroad, like exports do, and generate good jobs for low-income citizens. The government could help more hotels with incentives to better serve their employees, guests and sustain a great image of their region.

We know the retention levels usually are not high in lodging accommodation providers. It is not necessarily a must that the employees need to stay too long at the job, but a way to ensure hotels don't lose many employees is to provide job rotation programs among different departments inside hotels, such as marketing, sales, front desk, food and beverage, maintenance, security, landscaping and more. It has been proven to keep employees engaged and prepared for management positions with a broader overview of the entire operations.

On the economic level and how to be financially sustainable, hotels can act in many ways, but first, it needs to be reasonably profitable in the long term, otherwise, the disruptions are significant. For that, it requires proper management of financials via properly preparing reports such as income statements and balance sheets to monitor the financial performance and apply necessary adjustments timely.

Real Estate businesses like hotels require many times a mortgage and a lot of reserved funds to replace items in the future. To allow proper cash flow and enough to sustain day-to-day operations, such as paying employees on time, suppliers and on and on, it requires a combination of efforts from several fronts.

First on the revenue side with revenue managers in marketing and sales personnel bringing more revenues in the best way possible and then the expense and costs personnel also and like cost controllers. Therefore, leading to less waste. With the 20/80 rule, cost controllers can focus on 20% of the things that impact 80% of the financials, but not the contrary for personal energy conservation purposes and high positive output. It is also essential to have good levels of governance and transparency, handlings taxes and compliance with laws and regulations to avoid severe penalties that could threaten the continuity of the business.

Hostels - Shared Rooms and Social Fun

Hostels, note there is an 's' in between, are a part of the hospitality industry that is very interesting, as it will be explained why ahead.

Usually, regular hotels naturally act towards upgrading all aspects of their offers over the years as more profit they make and start catering to more affluent travelers. On the other hand, hostels, which are properties that offer shared rooms and more options to socialize for solo travelers, target the most price-sensitive customers that are many times young or traveling long-term.

Hostels do so by offering shared lodging accommodations with bunk beds that are known to be the cheapest in the industry, many times for less than $ 10 US dollars per single bed per night. Keep in mind that despite the low rates, these properties can have a higher profitability per space due to their higher volume. Hostels cater mostly to young adult solo travelers, many in their university gap years, digital nomads, backpackers, despite older flashpackers and business travelers are getting to enjoy the concept.

Solo traveling, when preferred, is usually due to the freedom of doing so when compared to traveling accompanied and having to adapt to other people's schedules and desires. Traveling solo also allows for more self-reflection time and fewer distractions to experience the destinations fully. Many guests seek socialization and parties. Maybe the only downside is that ground transportation such as Uber, Lyft and taxis charge per trip and not per person, therefore, solo travelers cannot share the cost of the ride, all the rest of the traveling costs are usually charged per person.

Some hostels can even charge from $30 to $50 per single bunk bed where there is not much competition or in rooms with lower occupancy capacity, such as 4 or 6 single bunk beds. There are female-only shared rooms and sometimes rooms with ensuite private bathrooms. In addition to that, many hostels offer an upscale experience in central locations, also known as 'poshtels', a combination of the words 'posh' and 'hostels' to indicate boutique hotels with shared accommodations. Another option known as Bposhtels is a hybrid pioneer new concept that brings aspects of hostels to hotels, without changing the hotels' main characteristics. Many solo travelers that could afford private rooms decide to stay in these shared rooms with other hostel-like amenities, such as social and fun activities due to their unique and valuable offerings, while enjoying more upscale amenities regular hotels offer.

How many people travel alone? Statistics on solo traveling are difficult to find and often data is not collected. Of course, not everybody that travels alone stays in hostels, but solo travelers frequently travel though, around three or more times a year and make up around 10% of the overall travel market. It is also important to differentiate between business, family-related, leisure and educational solo traveling.

Solo travel overall has been trending upwards since 2016, and many travelers are women, the overall trend shows a percentage growth of 131% in google searches for 'solo travel' and

Instagram hashtag #solotravel was associated with 5.2 million posts, per research from Condor Ferries in 2020.

Many people that are in transition in their lives, such as moving apartments or thinking of permanently moving to another city, prefer to stay in hostels for one, two or even three months due to their central locations, costs and social interactions. Guests also exchange useful information with others in the same situation, unlike in any other place. Plus, the fun of staying in these properties is unique since it can be a sociology class. Guests often form life-long friendships. Hostels are also offering more wellness activities and remote work infrastructure to capture these trends that skyrocketed after the Covid-19 pandemic. When compared to renting private apartments or houses for the same cost, the benefits of hostels are many, as compared below:

	Shared Rooms / Hostels	Private Apartments/Houses
Flexibility Daily - Easy In/Out Hotel/Hostel - No Term Contract		
Don't Depend on Other Roommates to Share the Rent		
Can Change to Another Room Easily if Don't Like Roommates		
Central Location for Public Transportation Walking Distance to Restaurants/Pharmacies/Markets		
Daily Housekeeping		
Linen Replaced by Housekeeper Every 7 Days		
Daily Fresh Towels	✔	✖
Fast Wi-Fi Included		
Toiletries (Shampoos, Soaps, Toilet Paper, Coffee, more)		
Breakfast Included Most Times		
24h Reception to Assist with Anything		
Make a LOT of Friends of the Same Age From All Over the World Helping Each Other		
Daily Social Calendar Activities to Have Fun		
Personal Large Storage with Padlocks		
All Utilities Included (Water, Energy, Trash)		

The concept of sharing a room with "stranger" roommates is not very known in some parts of the world and local building regulations don't even recognize or mention their existence, which makes it difficult for the development of these types of shared accommodations of bedrooms and bathrooms.

Airbnb, despite not focusing on shared accommodations with other "stranger" guests, also faced and still faces cultural barriers. When Airbnb was born back in 2007, people thought the idea sounded crazy, thinking strangers would never stay in each other's homes. But in the last 14 years, there have been over 1 billion guest arrivals on Airbnb. And every day, Airbnb claims to host over half a million "strangers". As it turns out, *'strangers aren't really that strange'* in recent commercials to stimulate more people try hosting.

The hostel industry is getting more recognized though and accepted as a viable and important part of the travel world, especially because it helps to introduce young adults to a cost-effective way of traveling, offers them ways to enjoy independence and better understand or accept other cultures. The fact that shared rooms are not yet fully understood also leads to huge misconceptions about these properties, guest types, safety and cleanliness. Many of these misconceptions are rectified once travelers see online pictures, read reviews and stay.

The future also relies on sharing and this type of hospitality allows many that could not afford to travel yet to experience it. Despite certain shared rooms misconceptions, there are more than 15,000 properties worldwide offering shared accommodations, 37% in Asia, 30% in Europe and 16% in South America. North America counts with less than 10%, according to data from the hostelhelper.com.

Several hospitality brands are targeting the younger generation of travelers and expanding despite most do not offer shared rooms. For example, Accor is set to bring 1,300 Jo&Joe hotels to China starting in 2023 just as an example. Other trendy hospitality brands are The Standard with 8 locations, The Student Hotel with 15, Citizen M with 25 and Moxy from Marriott with 111. However, many of these locations charge high rates.

Below from thehostelhelper.com are the largest hostel chains with shared rooms and related insights:

No.	Hostel Chain Name	Number Of Properties	Number Of Beds
#1	a&o Hostels	39	28,500
#2	Zostel	37	2,000
#3	Meininger	30	14,700
#4	St Christopher's Inns	26	3,700*
#5	Nomads World	25	n/a
#6	Hostel One	17	1,000
#7	Mad Monkey Hostels	15	1,200
#7	Generator	15	8,100
#9	Che Lagarto	14	n/a
#10	goSTOPS	13	850
#10	K's House	13	n/a
#10	Safestay	13	4,300
#13	Vietnam Backpacker Hostels	10	n/a
#14	Tribe Theory	9	n/a
#15	Nest Hostels	8	n/a
#15	Mad Monkey	8	n/a
#17	Pirwa Hostels	7	n/a
#17	Oasis Backpackers Hostels	7	n/a
#17	MacBackpackers	7	n/a
#20	Loki Hostels	6	n/a
#20	Hostels HUB	6	700*
#21	Astor Hostels	5	n/a
#21	Wombats	5	2,500
#21	Samesun Hostels	5	n/a
#21	Lub D Hostels	5	n/a
#25	Freehand	4	1,000
#25	Bohemian Hostels	4	n/a

#25	USA Hostels	4	725
#25	Hatters Hostels	4	n/a
#25	Smart Hostels	4	n/a
#30	Wake Up Hostels	3	n/a
#30	Pariwana Hostels	3	n/a
#30	Flying Pig Hostels	3	n/a
#30	Clink Hostels	3	1,500
#30	Plus Group	3	2,000
#30	Urbany Hostels	3	n/a
#30	Be Hostels	3	n/a
#30	Destination Hostels	3	283
#30	Funky Hostels	3	n/a

Hostelling International (HI), Selina and Young Hostels Association (YHA) consider themselves "hostel networks" not "hostel chains", therefore not present in the list above. In hostel networks, pretty much every independently operated hostel can join or leave networks while still being completely independent. It works like a membership. Sometimes hostel owners have to meet certain criteria or pay a fee to join these networks. The main benefit for hostels is that these platforms have large marketing budgets and provide another opportunity to receive direct bookings with their integrated booking engine.

By far, the largest hostel network is the non-profit association Hostelling International (HI) with more than 4,000 hostels in over 85 countries. In the United States and some other countries, HI fully owns hostels though and still operates many times as non-for-profit organizations with tax benefits. Selina claims 150+ locations in 25 countries and 42,000+ bed spaces, became a public company recently and is developing in a very fast pace with an interesting concept and initiatives.

However, the takeaway here is that the biggest regular hotel chain has more than 207 times the locations than the biggest hostel chain, and the hostel industry is still in the infancy stage with an extreme growth phase yet to come. Since hostels solve a basic need for lodging accommodation, it is safe to say that this industry is going to have a long growth and maturity stage. A decade ago, none of the hostel chains mentioned above had more than ten properties and I won't be surprised to see hostel chains with more than a hundred properties by 2030.

Timeshare Rough Path

The timeshare or vacation ownership industry model is a new concept when compared to other lodging types and faces challenges that are difficult to solve. In the following paragraphs, assuming readers have a basic knowledge of what the timeshare industry offers, I will disclose and analyze these challenges a bit harshly with the intention to create interest for improvements as areas of opportunity.

A timeshare is a type of vacation property with a shared ownership model. With a typical timeshare, owners and members share the cost of vacation properties, usually known as resort villas, with other buyers, and in return, they receive a guaranteed amount of time at their portfolio of owned or affiliated properties each year. For those that do not want to costly maintain standalone regular vacation properties that many times stay empty most of the year, the concept is brilliant.

It is well known, though, that the industry is going through a public relations crisis and a good number of unsatisfied owners or members continue, through a difficult process, to cut their relationships with their timeshare companies, mostly due to the difficulty in finding the desired availability and increases in their annual maintenance fees. Timeshare companies' representatives, such as the American Resort Development Association (ARDA) though claim via studies that the customer satisfaction levels are above 85%, according to the U.S. Shared Vacation Ownership Consolidated Owners Report, 2018 Ed conducted by Leger for the AIF and promoted by the association.

Of course, there are many timeshare companies, and each offers different products, prices and contract agreements. However, the topics below are somehow average and common practice among all players. The annual maintenance fee, normally paid ahead of time right after Christmas bills, ranges from $800 to $2,400 for the right to stay one week in a 2-bedrooms villa and is often subject to 10% yearly increases. If divided by seven days, this maintenance fee is slightly cheaper than regular resorts' daily rates for two double rooms. Cruises are even cheaper. However, the timeshare villas are very spacious.

To join, there is an average upfront cost of $25k or a financing option of 10-year with high annual interest rates of around 15% (house mortgages or cars usually have interest rates of 4%); this money could be invested in current or for other future high-quality resort stays.

Many times, it is also cheaper to rent timeshare villas than buy timeshare memberships. This is because timeshare companies offer cheaper stays to entice first-time buyers, or current owners rent their right of use. Long-term financial savings, one of the biggest selling arguments, is naturally blurry to calculate.

Besides that, timeshares have a minimum resale value and the secondary market is disorganized and risky. It is hard to exit the commitments even if you want to donate it. If owners or members don't pay any of their dues within 30 days, it can negatively affect more than 100 points their credit scores. Despite that, delinquency dazes the industry. Another issue is that the points used to trade for stays are subject to a loss of trading value. Because of all that, other companies are fraudulently deceiving owners and members, promising easy exits, and often these owners and members are elderly with financial struggles.

Many challenges are visible when comparing timeshares to regular resorts or cruises. Timeshare usually doesn't have daily housekeeping nor included food and beverages. Bigger and cheaper spaces with kitchens, one of the main selling points of timeshares, are now being offered by several regular resorts and vacation homes. Cruises include a vast array of food and beverage with their rates.

Timeshare owners and guests also need to reserve their stay many months ahead of time in order to guarantee desired dates and locations, which goes on the opposite trend of current travel patterns of booking very close to arrival dates. Travel habits are changing due to technological accessibility, even among older generations.

Also, when staying in regular resorts or cruises, customers are not enticed to go through a long and sometimes high-pressure sales presentation at the beginning of their vacations, as it happens in timeshare resorts. If owners buy or upgrade due to an oversight, the rescission period is not much longer than their current stay there, which we all know is difficult to ponder carefully while on vacation.

The industry is also trying to sell to younger-than-40-year-old generations, but would they like to share the resorts with an older generation of guests, which dominates the scene? Today the younger generation *wants access, not ownership*. Even reducing the upfront costs, usage period, or splitting annual maintenance fees into monthly payments, is unlikely to attract many new younger customers. On top of that, if the main demographics of customers pitched have kids, and if these kids are teenagers, the chances they don't want to travel with you are high, much less stay in the same villa. When they grow up, they won't like to inherit the timeshare financial obligations.

Timeshare is also difficult and expensive to sell, as the industry sales personnel likes to say, 'nobody wakes up desiring to buy a timeshare.' Now, with separate financial statements and required disclosures (the consequence of recent spin-offs from major hotel brands that also happened to reduce image risks), it is easier to see that the cost of sales and marketing, not even development or construction, is around 50% of total revenues, and for every ten prospects customers pitched (and gifted), only one ends up buying it.

Lastly, the industry also faces many regulation challenges and different particularities to develop and operate internationally and in each of the states in the United States where it is predominant.

All the challenges in the paragraphs above are intrinsic and difficult to solve. If the industry doesn't change to be more customer-centric, despite the already low-profit margins, it can face issues to grow.

Ways to improve can be by adopting best practices from other lodging accommodation providers like all-inclusive resorts, better exploring the timeshare's unique features, working on the industry's public image with PR firms, trying new ways to allow customers to better connect with each other, offering more attractions to younger generations such as extreme sports and nightclubs, reducing the financial burden to consumers and being more transparent and conscious of its costs, such as the high costs to sell timeshare and to operate or renovate the resorts that ultimately are repassed to its owners and members.

The timeshare industry has the potential to be extraordinary not only in the United States but internationally. It is still a new industry and therefore makes me believe it still has many opportunities to adapt, innovate and improve. One of the ways to achieve all this is by trying new approaches and taking risks, as some of the industry players are already starting to do it.

A Truly All-Inclusive Benchmark - The Club Med Case

Club Med built and sustains a unique, high-quality all-inclusive offer that has by far not been matched by other lodging providers.

I decided to expose their case in this material because after years of experience, I judge them to be very well-positioned and a great example of prime hospitality. The company did not sponsor me for writing this chapter, nor did it know my initiative and intention.

Club Med first saw the light of day in 1950 and was the result of a groundbreaking idea: offer vacations that combine sports with nature and the great outdoors in a relaxed and informal setting. Founded by the former Belgian water polo champion Gérard Blitz, Paris-based Club Med *pioneered the all-inclusive resort model* back in 1950 in Mallorca, Spain.

Club Med is a French travel and tourism operator headquartered in Paris, specializing in all-inclusive holidays. Club Med either wholly owns or operates nearly eighty all-inclusive resort villages in holiday locations around the world. They became very famous for mountain ski resorts but also for summer and beach locations. From 2001 onward, the resort company worked to rebrand itself as upscale and family oriented. In February 2015, Fosun International Ltd.'s Gaillon Invest II and The Silverfern Group finalized a challenging takeover deal of Club Méditerranée S.A. The Gaillon Invest's chairman, Jiannong Qian, believes that Chinese ownership of the company is crucial to tap into China's huge population of potential tourists. Following the takeover, the french Chairman and President of Club Méditerranée SA, Henri Giscard d'Estaing, was named President of Club Med SAS.

I have stayed in *numerous* all-inclusive resorts, of different brands, in different countries, and in different stages of my life, and I judge, after staying many times too at different Club Med resorts, that they offered the best overall experiences. After much thought, research and critical analyses, I have come to conclusions of why and how, which I will try to explain below, including interesting facts about them.

Most of their all-inclusive resorts share a formula of a truly fully immersive experience from all human senses' perspectives. Most of the time, you will interact with the right subset of guests and staff, usually filtered by cultural, educational and income levels, and attracted by their well-crafted marketing proposition. Also, their unique ambiance, from their large and often slightly remote locations within 1-hour drive from airports or larger cities, generates a distinctive atmosphere.

You will also experience a truly all-inclusive offer, where you do not need to pay on the spot for quality food, beverages (including alcoholic beverages), entertainment, child supervision, activities, sport instructions (many times unique, such as trapeze and water sky) and equipment.

Many of the multicultural staff (called Gentils Organisateurs or G.Os®) that interact with the guests live at the resort and are stimulated to engage with guests in a deeper way we don't encounter in other resorts. They long walk you to your rooms at check-in, sit at the same dining tables, have drinks together, are well dressed, dance together, take care of your kids during most of the day (in the way your kids like it and in groups) and practice sports together.

The way guests interact with each other and with the staff is carefully well-orchestrated in a great positive way during eating, drinking, the practice of sports, and live entertainment, such as during shows and nightclubs. It does take the guest-to-guest value co-creation to a very desirable level. Since the resorts attend greatly to most human needs, from the perspective of Maslow's hierarchy of human necessities, but also include pleasurable visual aspects from every corner, the guests spend valuable time socializing in their preferable ways with family, friends, staff, and other guests.

I judge cruises as the main competitors of Club Med, but they still lack many important aspects described above. Club Med, like cruises though, charges guests fully before check-in, which is not common in hotels or resorts. Weeklong packages are preferable, but they also sell weekends long rates. Interesting aspects of Club Med are also that they do not use OTAs to sell their nights but mostly sell directly from its website, via direct calls or via well-pampered travel agents. I don't remember any other lodging accommodation provider that opted only for this channel mix strategy, especially knowing the large number of rooms they have. Likely due to their quality, it is quite remarkable how they sustain themselves mostly on word-of-mount and repeated guests.

From their publicly available financial statements before the takeover, the company did not enjoy the same profit margins as some American hotels or resort chains, and I attribute that to the high quality offered and value for the money customers had. Their price ranges were not cheap though, especially after positioning themselves in the more upscale segment.

Interestingly too, is that Club Med is not very well known in the United States, in my view due to the differences between French/Chinese and American hospitality cultures. The company does not offer many locations in the United States, which is still a mystery to me why. I believe Americans are not exposed enough to Club Med, and if they were more, I would be curious to see how future experiences would go.

Guests' Journey Before, During and After their Hotel Stay

I invite hoteliers to look outside their properties at the entire journey and experiences guests have before, during and after their hotel stay, which are not necessarily controlled by the hotel but could be somehow or have at least their perceptions influenced by the hotel.

These include what triggers the necessity and the planning for the stay, how the planning occurs and who is responsible for it, how easy it is to convince others to join, how they obtain visas, passports, vaccines, insurance, luggage, clothes, etc., how is the infrastructure of airports, bus terminals, subways and roads, how they handle the several transportations, how will they pay for all, what surrounds the hotel or are nearby that guests also experience, how is security and cleanliness outside. And once they leave, how they keep remembering their memories related to the overall experience, plus how and when they decide to come back.

These, as you can see, are many, involving several stakeholders, and despite being extremely difficult to control, they affect the overall experience and will likely affect how your hotel is ultimately perceived.

Many believe that convenience is the ultimate goal, trying to interfere in this journey to cause an overall positive impact on travelers and save them from hassles. It is already a challenge to manage the hotel itself and there is also an excitement, unique of traveling, from the initial desires, from the planning and from the sharing of the good or bad experiences and memories after. The challenges encountered by travelers throughout the journey, when overcome, become a reason for pride.

Overall, traveling is many times leaving your comfort zone in pursuit of a greater prize. We can observe these stories that bad experiences turn out to be very positive experiences when, for example, backpackers describe their trips to South America or Asia, which, many times, despite the hassles, turn out to be very exciting experiences they relate to and brag about throughout their entire lives.

Of course, there are age and adventure factors to those who seek such traveling experiences. Most times, families or business travelers want the most convenient and relaxing travel experience they can encounter, however, of course, there is a higher price to pay for such convenience in most cases.

What is important from the hotelier's perspective is that despite all the challenges usually encountered by travelers, the hotel itself can be a midpoint oasis in facilitating the journey. With small gestures, pro-activeness and anticipation, hoteliers can deliver beyond what guests expect, even though when guests are aware the hotelier has no easy direct control over such external factors.

To give some examples, hoteliers can and should:

- Be in an attractive location, as obvious as it sounds
- Provide online guidance on what is required by local governments, such as vaccines

- Provide great directions to the hotel and with details about costs, transportation options and more
- Partner with transportation providers
- Post fair pictures of what to expect outside and inside
- Provide easy ways to pay for the services, such as automatic online charges, etc.
- Partner with nearby businesses to accomplish and or demand better infrastructure, security and cleanliness surrounding the hotel
- Partner with local businesses to promote each other by offering mutual benefits, such as discounts in restaurants, shuttles, theme parks, retails and more
- Communicate with a sample of guests via email or phone/text preferably to ask if everything went ok. Ideally, also offering a way of keeping the experience in memory, such as a small, personalized souvenir or picture of their stays.

We know looking outside the hotel and the guests' entire journey is difficult. Only the hoteliers organized enough and in a good position financially will have the time and privilege to research, plan and try to interfere with these journeys. I hope that can become more and more common and leave the last note to invite hoteliers to always have in their minds the interest in being involved with these external factors.

www.ingramcontent.com/pod-product-compliance
Lightning Source LLC
Chambersburg PA
CBHW051357150726
48000CB00003B/1218